Urban Textures | Yves Lion

Jean-Louis Cohen

Principal photography:
Gitty Darugar
Jean-Marie Monthiers
Adrià Goula Sarda

Birkhäuser Publishers for Architecture
Basel · Berlin · Boston

Contents

Page 2: Porte des Lions, new entrance to the Musée du Louvre, Paris, 1999, stairs leading to the Department of Painting.

Right: Palace of Justice, Lyons, 1995, south façade.

Introduction

A mélange of genres

Firmly anchored within the fourteenth arrondissement of Paris since the mid 1970s, Yves Lion has left his mark on Parisian architectural culture both by the texture of several of his buildings and by his personal experience. But the place he occupies in European architecture of the past twenty years is as original as it is difficult to define due to his unusual ability both to adhere to and transcend the spirit of Paris — and furthermore to his ability to work with extremely diverse scales and urban situations. While his positions and his fights are shaped by consistency and persistence, they do not lean on a dogmatic reflection dictating their methodical implementation. They nevertheless reflect the major issues discussed in the debates on architecture, urban form and landscape that have taken place in Europe since 1980 and are to be seen within in this frame.

Within fifteen years, a period marked by positive reception almost more intense in Spain, Germany and Italy than in France, Yves Lion twice received the *Équerre d'Argent* Prize as a reward for the most outstanding building of the year. Between the extension of the Museum of Franco-American Cooperation at Blérancourt, designed in cooperation with Alan Levitt and awarded in 1989, and the French Embassy in Beirut, designed in cooperation with Claire Piguet and premiated in 2003, his production was the object of numerous individual analyses, but was presented rarely in the context of his overall activities, his permanent patterns and his hesitations. During this period his work underwent strong expansion and perceptible metamorphosis. Two monographs published in 1985 and 1992 paid great attention to the office's early buildings, offering a useful primary frame of interpretation that provided a scale of the transformations at work in its production.[1]

His deployment towards a new scale of work and new programmes now requires other forms of interpretation. Yves Lion's early commissions for public buildings were won in architectural competitions, but subsequently his work branched out and adjusted to a more complex reality. His contribution to reflections on public housing and his own work drew particular attention towards contact with multiple local authorities in the practice of the particular understanding of urban design known in France as a *projet urbain*. It would be tempting to read this contribution according to an essentially typological grid, a reading undoubtedly clear as well as effective; however, the course to be followed here will be another, tending to draw evidence from the original strategic decisions that shape Lion's work at its various dimensions in the long-term. Before looking at a wide range of architectural works, a historical detour is necessary in order to understand the interweaving of episodes during Yves Lion's itinerary and the circumstances that have shaped French and European architectural culture over the past four decades. Indeed, if there are recurring attitudes and themes, his architecture is no less determined by the phases of an eventful history in terms of architectural ideals, of public policy and of architectural commissions.

1. *Yves Lion* (introduction by Alexandre Chemetoff, interview with Pierre-Alain Croset), (Barcelona: Gili, 1992); *Yves Lion: études, réalisations, projets, 1974–1985* (Paris: Electa Moniteur, 1985), presentation by Daniel Treiber.

Museum of Franco-American Cooperation, Blérancourt, 1989, view from the arboretum.

French Embassy, Beirut, 2003, entrance.

The architect's design concepts are difficult to dissociate from the experience he acquired on both sides of the Mediterranean, between his "homeland" France and his "country," Morocco. His childhood was spent in Casablanca during the decade prior to Moroccan independence, where his mother worked in one of the numerous Modernist buildings in a city that was experiencing an authentic golden age in architecture. His father, a photographer, specialised in sports journalism.[2] An inventor of an ingenious system for catching the finishing line on film, he allowed his son to accompany him during the summers to follow the Tour de France.

As a permanent building site Casablanca was undeniably an architectural learning place for the young boy. He lived in the Rue Lamoricière and attended the Alphonse Daudet School, in the vicinity of the Rue de l'Aviation Française, built for the main part during the 1930s. These Art Deco buildings were dwarfed by the large modern building of the Cité Maréchal Foch, which housed high-ranking officers of the French military.[3] The roofs of the garages and cinemas, and the terraces of the buildings, provided unlimited playing grounds. Casablanca was an exceptional architectural landscape punctuated by outstanding buildings, and was also the showground for the conflicts leading to Moroccan independence, in which the city played a vital role as told in Tito Topin's detective stories.[4] Festive celebration of decolonization and the influx of Moroccans into the centre from which they had until then been kept at bay, and, following independence, their subsequent discovery of beaches created for Europeans, led to the young man's understanding of the pluralist nature of the world.

A silent nostalgia for Morocco made Yves Lion impatient while attending Paris' secondary schools during the 1960s; he thus decided to plunge into the world of architectural offices at a time when the construction of high-rise housing schemes was at its height. He worked with Jack Hamoniau, designer of large developments for the Caisse des Dépôts et Consignations and established contacts with several of Hamoniau's colleagues. But the discoveries of *L'Art décoratif d'aujourd'hui* (*The Decorative Art of Today*) and of *Vers une architecture* (*Towards a New Architecture*), which Le Corbusier had republished before his death in 1965, provided him with another view of architecture, encouraging him to apply for his *baccalauréat* as a free candidate. Henceforth he was able to enter one of the ateliers in preparation of the admission test to the École des Beaux-Arts in Paris. He did not join the atelier run by Georges Candilis, a central figure in the deployment of reformist policies in the school but was accepted by Georges-Henri Pingusson, a notable figure in architecture and modern urban planning who had been active in occupied Saarland and Lorraine after the War, and who had just completed the Deportation Memorial in Paris.

2. Roger Lion is one of the heroes of a popular detective story staged during the Tour du Maroc cycling race: Marcel-E. Grancher, *La Belle de Bousbir* (Paris: Éditions Rabelais, 1956).

3. See their analysis in: Jean-Louis Cohen, Monique Eleb, *Casablanca, Colonial Myths and Architectural Ventures* (New York: The Monacelli Press, 2002), p. 376–377.

4. Tito Topin, *55 de fièvre* (Paris: Gallimard, 1983); *Piano barjo* (Paris: Gallimard, 1983).

Pierre Jabin, Moretti-Milone Building, Casablanca, 1934.

Edmond Brion, Bendahan Building, Casablanca, 1934.

Léonard Morandi, "Liberté" Building, Casablanca, 1949.

David-Georges Emmerich and Students from the Unité Pédagogique n° 6, structures built in the courtyard of the École des Beaux-Arts, Paris, c. 1970.

The teaching of Pingusson, quite present among beginner students at the time, unlike most other professors, did not compensate for the archaisms of the school. Besides, like many of his contemporaries, Yves Lion was appalled by the American war in Vietnam. He became involved in the occupation of the Beaux-Arts and the creation of new schools.[5] He attended the *Unité Pédagogique n° 6*, led by many figures from the Parisian May Revolt, becoming acquainted with Antoine Grumbach and Jacques Lucan, figures of a more intellectual breed from the extreme left. Among the teaching staff he met Jean-Pierre Buffi who initiated him to the architectural discourses of Aldo Rossi and David Georges Emmerich, the genius inventor of three-dimensional structures. During a Summer Session at the Architectural Association in London in 1971 he discovered the Archigram utopians, such great figures of the "intellectualised" profession as James Stirling and Aldo van Eyck and young critics Charles Jencks and Bernard Tschumi. After 1968, French schools, and notably the UPA 6, were drifting away from the practice of architectural design; for Lion, the London experience counteracted this tendency, thus confirming his professional determination. From 1972 he swiftly concluded his curriculum with a diploma thesis tutored by Buffi, with occasional Situationist accents. He studied the re-use of buildings, such as the Palace of Diocletian at Split, taking into account the analyses of Jacob Bakema, the conversion of the Daumesnil Railway Viaduct, in Paris, and of the San Francisco Cannery (Joseph Esherick, 1968), echoing the sociological analyses of Jane Jacobs. The thesis include a sketch proposal for the re-use of the Paris prison of La Petite Roquette, then meant to be demolished.[6]

From this time onwards he led a double life of sorts, revelatory of the new conditions in which French architecture and culture operated in the 1970s. The progressive and unstoppable increase in public architectural competitions was accompanied in the cultural domain by the creation of new institutions with unprecedented ambitions in terms of worldwide deployment, such as the Centre Georges Pompidou. Yves Lion was thus to successfully engage in professional practice under the new conditions of public commissioning, increasingly open towards outsiders and young people, but nonetheless he had to rely on funding provided by cultural institutions to make a living. With the experience and familiarity that he had enjoyed since childhood towards the world of photography he travelled all over Europe with his fellow-student Daniel (Hubert) Tajan, in order to assemble a stock of images for the colour-slide library of the Centre de Création Industrielle, a department for the Centre Pompidou, prior to its opening in 1977. This "grand tour" of a particular kind led him to discover Bruno Taut's Siedlungen (housing estates) in Berlin, the Viennese Höfe and the buildings of Alvar Aalto. He would never abandon this essential practice of photography, gathering notations and visual reflections during his travels and on building sites — in short learning "How to Look at Architecture," to put it in the words of the title of Bruno Zevi's work, one of the few foreign books available in French translation to students at the Beaux-Arts prior to 1968.[7]

5. For these episodes, see: Jean-Louis Violeau, *Les architectes et le mythe de mai 68* (Saint-Denis: Université de Paris 8, 2002), (doctoral thesis supervised by Monique Eleb).
6. Yves Lion, *Quelques exemples de détournement* (Paris: Unité pédagogique d'architecture n° 6, 1972) (diploma thesis supervised by Jean-Pierre Buffi).
7. Bruno Zevi, *Sapere vedere l'architettura* (Turin: Einaudi, 1948); English translation: *Architecture as Space: How to Look at Architecture* (New York: Horizon Press, 1957).

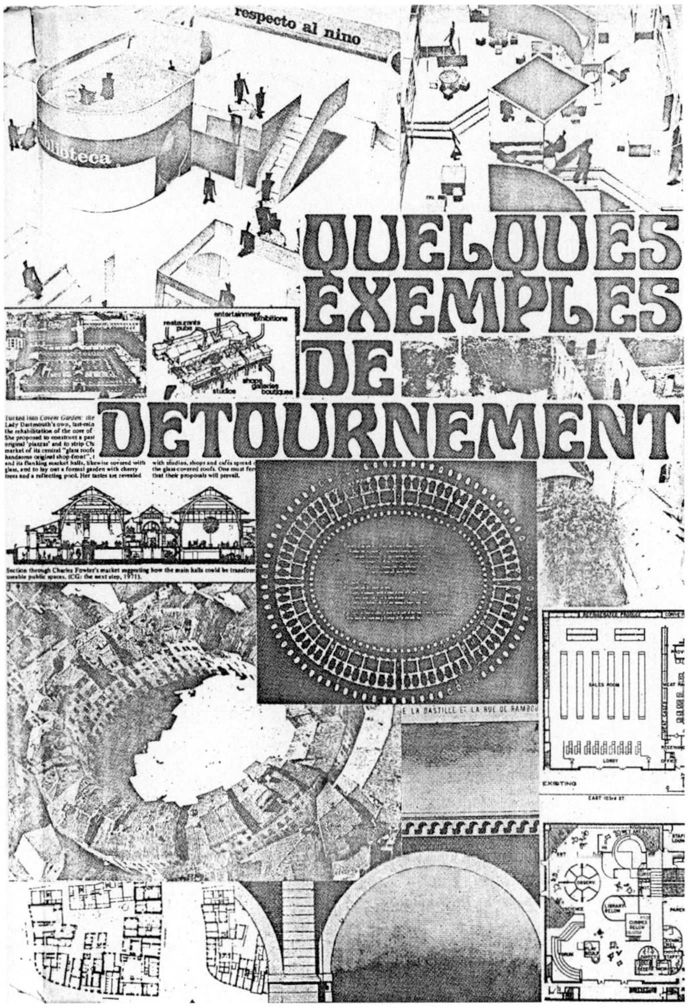

Yves Lion, architect's
diploma thesis, cover, 1972.

Bruno Taut, Freie Scholle
housing estate, Berlin, 1928.

Yves Lion was an assiduous participant in the competitions that encouraged his generation to become active after having rejected project involvement for several years; he participated in most confrontations marking the conceptual renewal of French architecture. Together with Jean-Paul Rayon he was successful in the first phase of the competition for the Maubuée Hills area in the new town of Marne-la-Vallée. On passing the second phase he joined a team consisting of, among others, Paul Chemetov, Edith Girard, Jacques Lucan and Fernando Montes, the team being named Eupalinos Corner. *L'Architecture d'aujourd'hui*'s chief editor Bernard Huet saw at the time in this project and that of its competitor AREA "two swallows perhaps making the summer." The team rejected the combinatory games that were fashionable at the time and the idea of a superficial "animation" of forms through the creation of artificial picturesque features, calling instead for the spirit of an "order" and an "aesthetic architectural strategy," the only one to "provide possible future usage."[8]

Triggered by the public bodies in charge of the building programme, in this inaugural case, team work, in a supple and changing configuration, became a constant of the Lion method. Certain teams would be numerous if not plethoric, such as Eupalinos Corner and, twenty years later, Hippodamos 93, constituted to develop the Saint-Denis Plain, a vast expanse of obsolete industrial fabric connecting Saint-Denis and the north of Paris, with Pierre Riboulet, Michel Corajoud, Philippe Robert and the DUT Group, all united after having refused to compete against each other; other teams were more fragile, such as the enigmatic and short-lived group 75021 formed in 1988 in order to study the urban destiny of Paris. Engaged in a permanent creative dialogue, some of the partners remained for a long time and became joint authors of projects, such as Tajan, Alan Levitt or, in the 1990s, Claire Piguet, who today is one of the associates of Lion's office along with Isabelle Chlabovitch, David Jolly, Sojin Lee and Étienne Lenack. With the landscape architect Alexandre Chemetoff the dialogue was maintained on a regular basis for a long time. Others were to be present at strategic points in time, such as Rayon, Daniel Treiber, Bernard Althabégoïty or Riccardo Rodinò (a man of unusual talent and extraordinary rationality who died prematurely), Henri Ciriani, François Leclercq or Marc Mimram. It was in the culture of sport, encountered during the Tour de France and on rugby fields that Yves Lion found the metaphors for this practice. Thus the image of football presented itself without effort when he recognised the importance of Ciriani's position of "centre-forward" although he added that other players were essential in order to make up a team.[9]

8. "Deux hirondelles font peut-être le printemps," *L'Architecture d'aujourd'hui*, No. 174, July/August 1974, p. 42–44.
9. Yves Lion, "Projets parisiens," *Paris d'architectes* (Paris: Éditions du Pavillon de l'Arsenal, 1996), p. 14–39 (lecture given on 2 February 1994), p. 17; see also: Yves Lion, "L'avant-centre," in: *Henri Ciriani* (Paris: Institut français d'architecture/Éditions du Moniteur, 1984), p. 17.

The studio in 1985. Left to right: Yves Lion, Jean-Luc Hesters, Daniel Tajan, Claire Piguet, Alan Levitt, Françoise Lion, Cathialine Althabégoïty, François Leclerq, Marie Malivel, Bernard Althabégoïty.

The "Eupalinos Corner" team at work on the Côteaux de Maubuée competition, 1974. Present on the photo: Vittorio Pisu, Daniel Tajan, Costas Kostakis, Jacques Lucan, the secretary, Felice Fanuele, Edith Girard, Paul Chemetov, the «Brazilian», Bernard Paurd, Fernando Montes, Jean-Paul Rayon, Yves Lion.

Competition for the Côteaux de Maubuée in Marne-la-Vallée, 1974, with Eupalinos Corner, regulating lines of the plan.

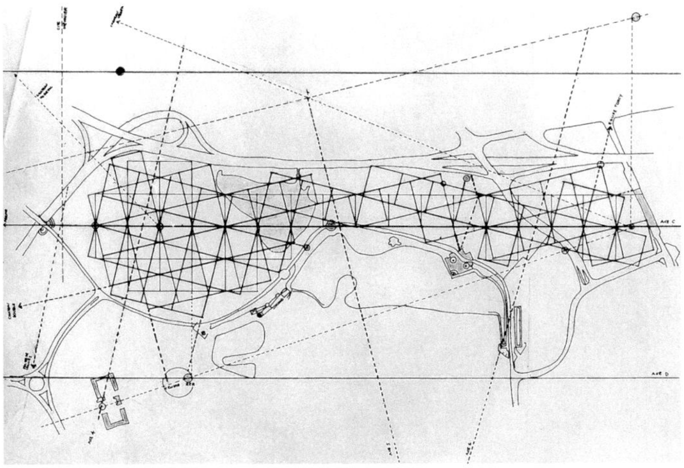

Before his first successes in architectural competition, followed, sometimes considerably later, by eventual construction, Yves Lion spent much energy on uncertain adventures initiated by French public authorities and indicating the way forward for new ideas in architecture. In 1974 he was the prize-winner in the seventh round of the *Programme architecture nouvelle*, an annual contest for emerging architects, whose contribution to a reappraisal of housing was fundamental. He participated in the competition for the grounds of the Petite Roquette in Paris (1974), in the first stage of the redevelopment of the former abattoirs of La Villette (1976) and in the competition organised by the Syndicat de l'architecture — an alternative professional union — for the development of Les Halles in Paris (1979). He entered competitions for the cathedral squares in Amiens (1975) and Orléans (1976), before winning further contests that led him, finally, to build the Law Courts in the southern city of Draguignan (1978) as well as in Lyons (1981), completed much later.

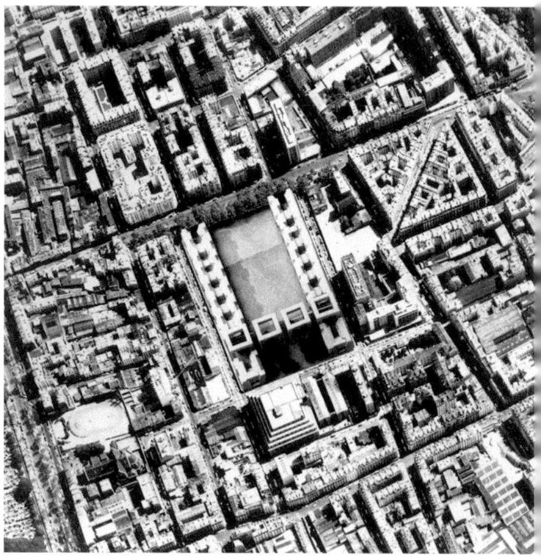

Competition for the grounds of the former Roquette jail, Paris, 1974, photomontage of the plan.

Competition for the square in front of the cathedral, Amiens, 1975, photomontage.

Palace of Justice, Draguignan, 1983, plan displaying the integration in the city.

Competition for the square in front of the cathedral, Orléans, 1976, elevation.

While working on these projects he remained in dialogue with the associates and friends mentioned above, elaborating the first elements of a vocabulary founded on a mastered conflict between orthogonal geometry and focus on the lines and irregularities of the site. A voluntary limitation of rhetorical effects and constructive clarity characterised these projects, often of a provocative nature, by their emphatic linearity such as in the school at Marne-la-Vallée or in the Les Halles project. Complexity then resulted from combining this approach with the particular local conditions, such as in Draguignan. In the first housing complexes built in the new town at L'Isle d'Abeau or in the old Atlantic port of Rochefort, the linear rows of houses constituted a primary order marked by the serial play of porches and openings. Aldo Rossi seemed to be in dialogue here with Bruno Taut.

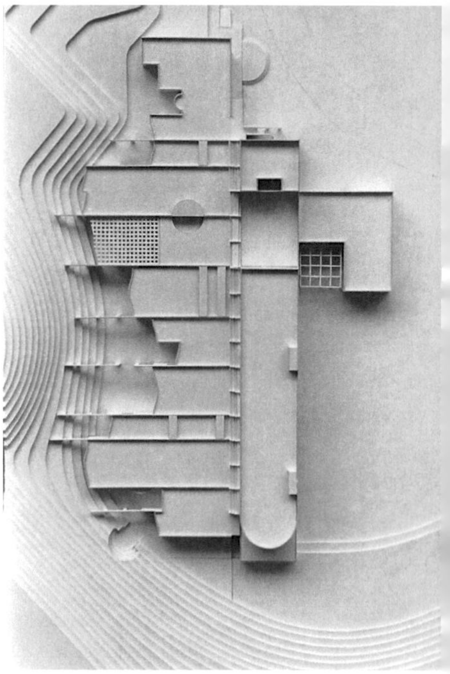

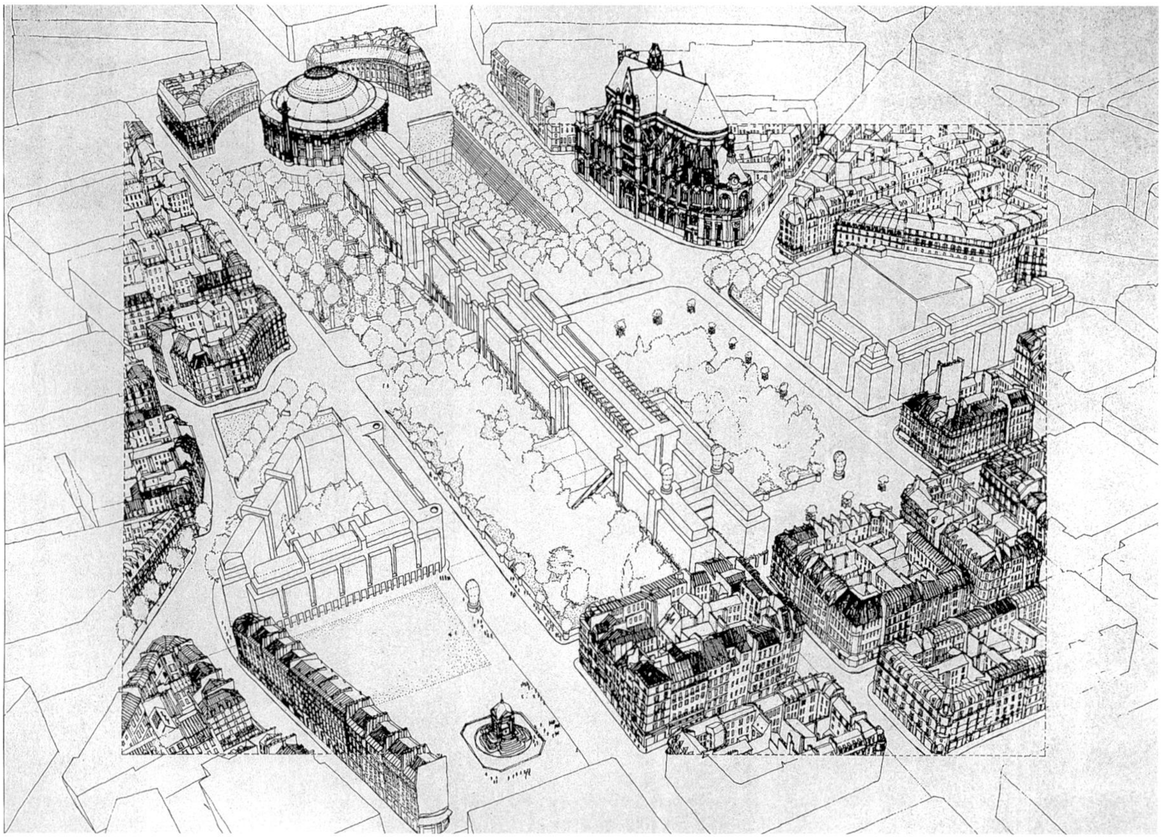

Competition for an elementary school, Marne-la-Vallée, 1977, view of the model.

International competition for the Les Halles area, Paris, 1979, perspective.

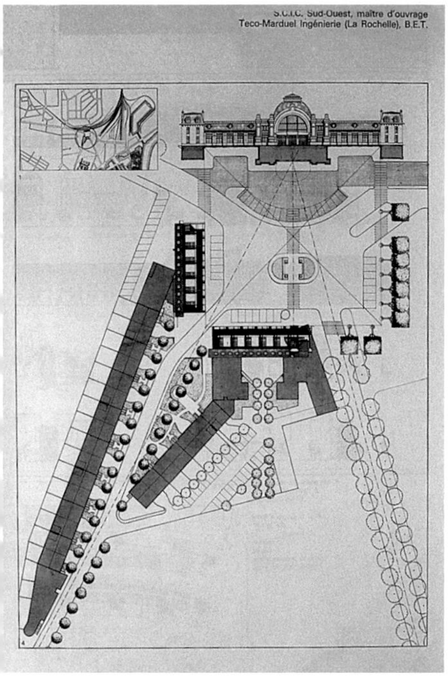

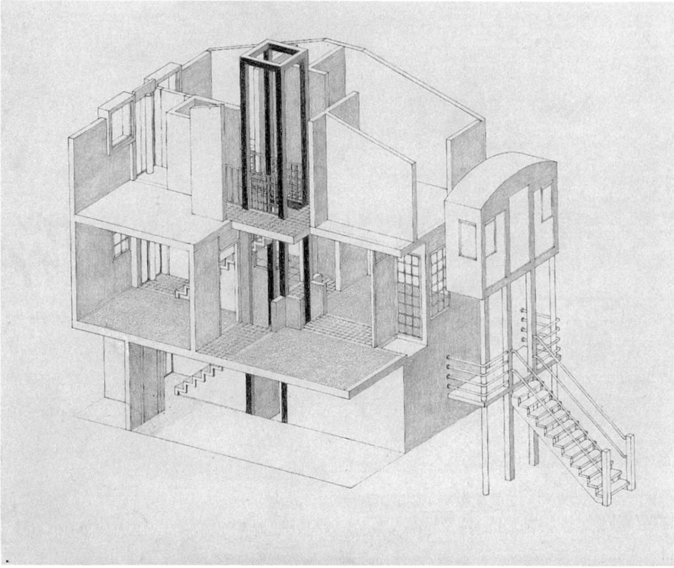

30 single-family houses, Rochefort-sur-Mer, 1982, massing plan.

66 single-family houses, L'Isle d'Abeau, 1981, structure of the houses, axonometric drawing.

30 single-family houses, Rochefort-sur-Mer, 1982, view from the street.

Parallel to this first generation of competition projects, Yves Lion discovered teaching, for him a constant domain of intellectual investment, but initially with an audience of engineers. In 1977 he was recruited by the École Nationale des Ponts et Chaussées when Paul Chemetov replaced Jean Balladur at the chair of architectural design. In familiarising his students with the methods of architectural conception he urged them to rethink the project dimension of their profession, at a time when economic or scientific aspects had been favoured — distinctly not Lion's attitude. While teaching at the École d'Architecture de Paris-Tolbiac between 1987 and 1998, he not only engineered the school's relocation to Champs-sur-Marne in the late 1990s, in a building conceived by Bernard Tschumi, but also the re-shaping of its programme. The accent put on issues of urban structuring and landscape gave the displaced school a definitely new identity. His contribution to the modernisation of education in France owed much during this phase to the experience acquired while teaching workshops in Canada and primarily at the École Polytechnique Fédérale in Lausanne, to which he was frequently invited as a visiting professor.

The first seven-year term of François Mitterrand (1981–1988) was a contradictory period for French architecture in many regards. The policy of *grands travaux* (great building projects) was merely the most spectacular aspect of a cultural development marked by an explosion of expositions and publications. But Yves Lion had only one limited success with the spectacular Paris competitions in which he was frequently a runner-up. He was one of the few invited to the limited competition for the Institut du Monde Arabe, and the large triangle he designed for La Défense in 1983 received honourable mention, whereas he had conceived at a previous stage a "filter" building for the same site. While his entry for the International Conference Centre at the Quai Branly (1989) had been ranked first by the jury, it was eventually turned down. This proved a bad omen as the entire project ended up being abandoned, before it was revived as a museum designed by Jean Nouvel.

Competition for the «Tête Défense», Paris, 1983, view from Paris (east) and view from the periphery (west).

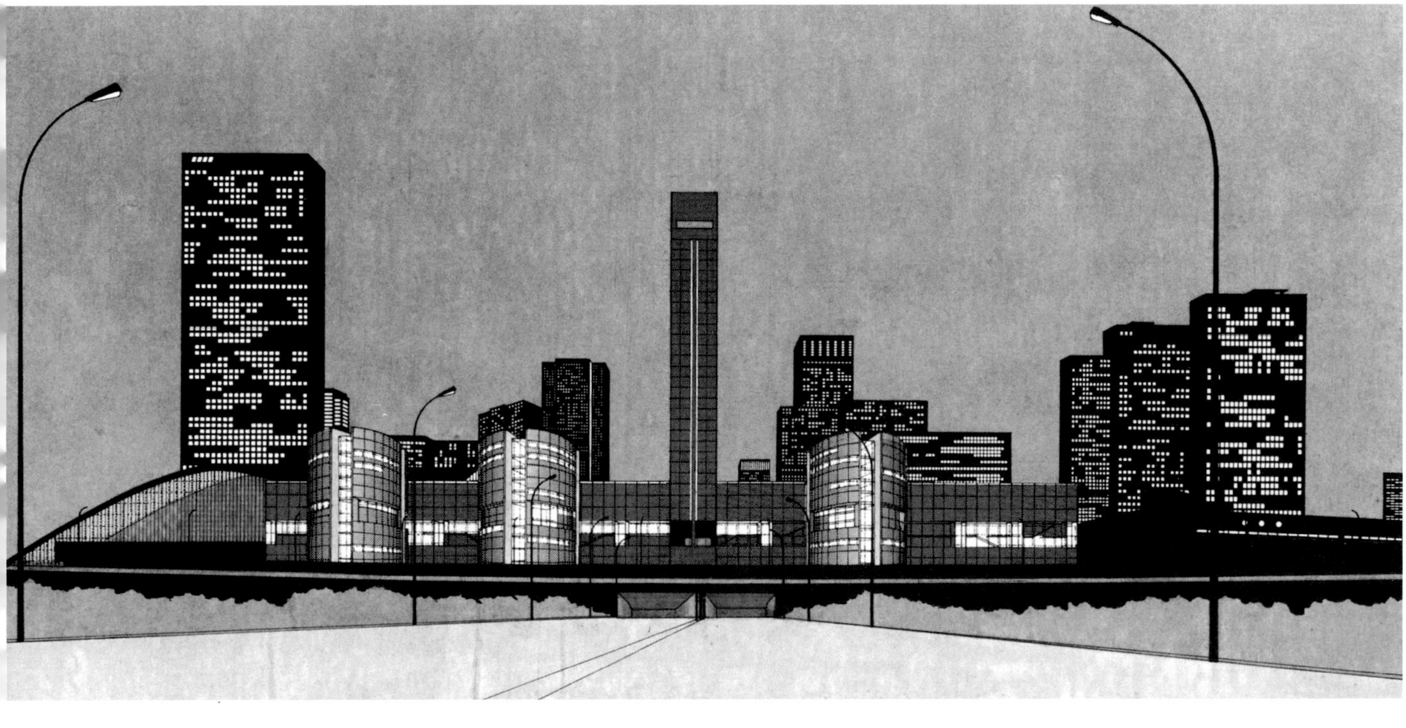

His work then turned to other adventures. His theoretical design, *Domus demain*, elaborated with François Leclercq, proposed between 1984 and 1988 an overall rethinking of the structure of multi-family housing in a revival of utopia developed while working on large housing projects in Paris and Noisy-le-Grand. The experience of the territorial scale of new towns and, moreover, his first building sites in the capital were milestones in the concrete experience of big-city landscapes. A milestone of a different sort would be the contract for the extension of the Blérancourt Museum, this time obtained without running a competition (the exception merely confirms the rule here!), thanks to museum curator Pierre Rosenberg's interest in a project by the Lion office for the Louvre that had been rejected. This extension inaugurated a series of buildings of a more intimate nature; its logic went beyond the playful manipulation of series and existing typologies. The building constructed for Lion's agency in the Rue Didot, with workshops and offices piled in a sandwich-like manner on top of one another and then wrapped in a case of marble, was on a comparable scale and, like the museum, distinguished itself by the assonance of its abstract geometry with the perforated pattern of adjacent masonry façades.

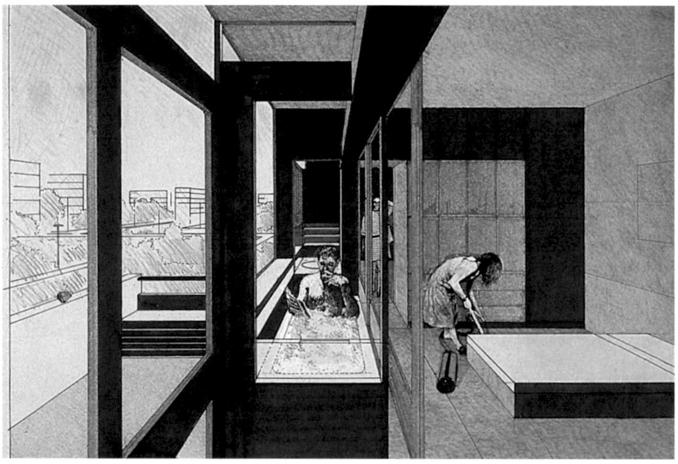

Housing scheme, Rue Liancourt, Paris, 14th arrondissement, 1995.

Domus demain project, bedroom and bathroom, 1984, perspective.

Lion architecture studio, Rue Didot, Paris, 14th arrondissement, 1989.

Artists' studios, Passage de Flandre, Paris, 19th arrondissement, 1987.

In 1995, the final version of the Law Courts in Lyons and the changes the design had undergone since winning the competition indicate the scale of transformations that this type of programme underwent in France. This transformation stemmed from the reflections of an innovative and attentive team on the part of the client and also demonstrated what had changed in the office's approach. The relation between the slab of the offices and the promontories of the audience halls was less mechanistic than in the initial design, the affinity between the building, whose floor area was cut down to half of the original plan, and the Part-Dieu quarter was more delicate and the palette of materials more sensitive, having expanded to include stone, metal and wood. The refinement of the cross-sections gave greater clarity to the inner circulation, while the intervention by Alexandre Chemetoff transformed the roofs of the rooms into a suspended, set-back garden. This was more than the inevitable streamlining of a project in the course of time; it was an experience of great operations condensing, just as it happened in the Convention Centre and the Opera completed in Nantes in 1992. In the latter case the differentiation of the project's two large spaces — the wood-clad cave of the foyer and the orthogonal exhibition areas as well as the auditorium on a circular plan — did not impair the unity of a project that was adapted to the site and to the complicated geometry of the Île de la Loire's existing fabric.

Great hall of the Convention Centre, Nantes, 1992, interior view.

Palace of Justice, Lyons, 1995, street view.

In the 1990s another metamorphosis occurred in the practice of the office, now grown confident in its ability to accomplish large architectural assignments. Lion affirmed: "I design simple forms because it is these I master best; it troubles me to see architects going beyond what they are capable of doing," and he went on to criticise "this official architecture [...] in which buildings are no longer subject to the context."[10] Addressing urbanistic aspects — often latent but also concrete in numerous designs of varied scale — became just as important as the building project itself in a political climate that was marked by the effects of decentralisation. Local authorities now empowered to establish their own planning processes started conceiving their "urban projects" and this gave a new responsibility to designers. The duration of building projects was sometimes prolonged, as they were repeatedly reoriented through political decisions, such as in the case of the Saint-Denis Plain development and later the construction of the Stade de France (by Macary, Zubléna, Régembal and Costantini) in 1993–1998. This phenomenon was evidence of an approach more receptive to local demand and perception. With the project for the redevelopment of Place Montcalm in Nîmes (1991) or large-scale endeavours such as the Cité de la Méditerranée in Marseilles and the Masséna-Bruneseau sector of the Paris-Rive-Gauche urban renewal scheme, both commissioned in 2002, a new approach emerged that was by no means a mechanical enlargement of building projects. This approach took its place in the considerable production of urban design studies commissioned by local authorities and developers; an impressive body of work ensued that remains, however, most difficult to scan, due to the inadequacy of record-keeping policies. The lack of orderly archives may result in a considerable amount of design work falling into oblivion.

10. Yves Lion, "Comment faire la ville? Entretien avec Yves Lion," *Les Cahiers de la recherche architecturale*, No. 32–33, 1993 (interview conducted by Jean-Jacques Treuttel), p.132.

Paris Rive-Gauche, Masséna-Bruneseau sector, 2001, perspective.

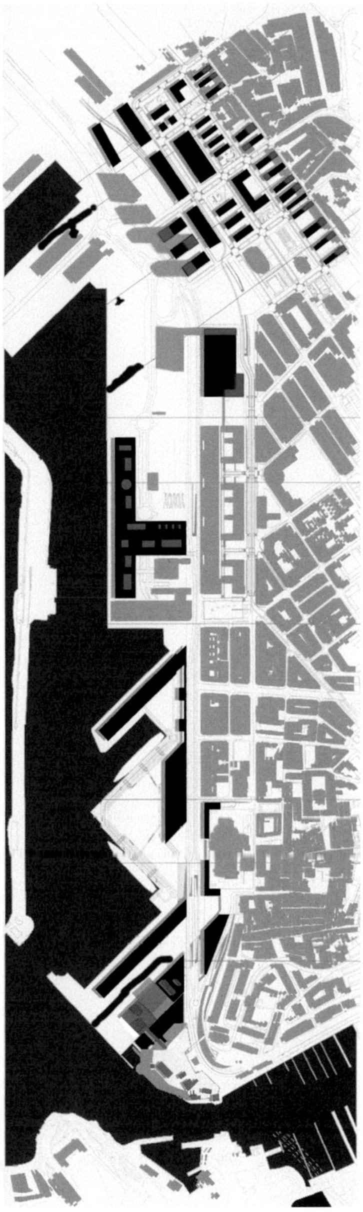

Cité de La Méditerranée, Marseilles, 2001, general plan.

Competition for the Montcalm Square, Nîmes, 1991, initial state and planned state.

During this new phase Yves Lion became more vocal, often in the form of interviews. He engaged particularly in public action going beyond the dialectics of individual projects. Between 1997 and 2001 he devoted much energy to the formation of the École d'Architecture de la Ville et des Territoires in Champs-sur-Marne. To the initial core of teaching staff, who had come from the Tolbiac School in Paris, he added new forces sharing, as put by a manifest in which the positions of Alexandre Chemetoff could be clearly perceived, the task of "moving the job of the architect towards the organisation of voids in between and their potential to include built space, completely sidestepping the disciplinary autonomy which architects long cherished but which often failed to establish true contact with the public or to attempt reconciliation."[11]

Yves Lion refuses to be seen as a theoretician and often makes a point of operating by instinct. Transposing his excellent knowledge of music to architecture and urban planning, beginning with jazz, he countered the emotion of the author or the artist with what he calls—according to a French anglicism—a "feeling" for places, their atmosphere and intuitive effects.[12] It is also this sensation that led him to take risks, such as working with original and talked-about clients like Apollonia, responsible for developments that were inventive in their spatiality and moreover in their mode of marketing, but which were denounced by some critics for their kitsch façades.[13] The projects in Marseilles and above all in Bordeaux (2002) did not fail to bring the interior organisation and the expression of the façade into alignment, a match strongly shaped by the developer's intention to obtain high-quality apartments, mostly in the form of maisonettes, and his specific commercial outlook. Another risk was quite simply that of public dialogue. Lion took up this challenge in November 2000 by assuming the leadership for the large audience encounter *Les rendez-vous de l'architecture* in La Villette on the theme of "*Transforma(c)tions.*" Deeply convinced of the power of words and direct relations between people of goodwill, he organised a confrontation between politicians, critics, urban planners, architects and landscape architects on the question of improving life in cities and of the participation of the cities' inhabitants.

11. Yves Lion, "Pour une nouvelle école d'architecture des territoires" in: Pierre-Alain Croset, ed., *Pour une école de tendance, mélanges offerts à Luigi Snozzi* (Lausanne: Presses polytechniques et universitaires romandes, 1999).
12. Yves Lion, interview with Soline Nivet, June 2002, published in: *La lettre de George V*, 2002.

13. Jacques Lucan, "Architectures fin de siècle," *Le Moniteur architecture AMC*, No. 112, December 2000/ January 2001, p. 186–189 (text from the lecture "L'érosion de l'architecture," given at *Les Rendez-vous de l'architecture*, 17 November 2000).

Jury discussion of the Tomato group's thesis, École d'Architecture de la Ville et des Territoires, Marne-la-Vallée, 1999.

Poster for the "Transforma(c)tions" conference, Paris, 2000.

A jazz aficionado as well as a connoisseur of Debussy or Shostakovich, Yves Lion is an equally eclectic reader of architectural history, which he approaches with similar openness and without the least fetishism. Sensitive to certain Le Corbusier buildings, such as those at Chandigarh, he was able to escape the monomaniac fixation of several of his contemporaries and build a very personal pantheon featuring Auguste Perret and Louis Kahn, but also Aldo Rossi (more due to his analyses than to his buildings), Alvaro Siza and Luigi Snozzi. Symptomatically, following his reports from the 1970s he retained his admiration for the "thousands of dwellings" built by Bruno Taut, in his eyes "the true modern architect, capable of abandoning his aspirations of style, his personal quests in order to design and build." Despite the fact that he "was misled in his association with the *Novembergruppe,* which wanted to radically change Man," he considered that Taut's "strong and exaggerated convictions did not prevent him from building humble and generous housing complexes."[14] Lion only subscribes to the discourse of the "Modern Movement" in this domain when it refuses the autonomy of forms, justifying his "affiliation to Ernst May or André Lurçat" since, for them, "façades have no other *raison d'être* than their rapport to the interior."[15] He later discovered the designs by the Sri Lankan architect Geoffrey Bawa; these had a profound effect upon him in that he appeared to identify with them and perceived them as an alternative to "high" history: "He doesn't bring about the battle of the classes. He does not change the world; but *he* is what changes. [...] He looks a lot towards Italy but doesn't appeal to the Pazzi for a Yes or for a No."[16]

Yves Lion's vision of the world can be understood through his photography as well as through his texts. As a medium of permanent observation, photography reveals his attention to landscape and the constructed detail and his ability to find spatial solutions that are not in the least heroic nor display a particular radicalism, but "work" properly. Here again there is no fetishism, as indicated by his commentaries on the pictures brought back from Sri Lanka: "Modern or ancient, whatever. With Bawa you can forget this question of so little pertinence in this context."[17] This "mélange of genres," which Lion has not ceased to call for, echoing the multiculturalism of the Morocco of his childhood, is also emblematic of his attitude towards the collective experience of twentieth-century architecture.

The image of a "lingua franca" was promoted by a joint exhibition at the gallery 9H in London in 1987, together with Patrick Berger and Pierre-Louis Faloci, architects sharing some of his beliefs. The exhibition's point was to underline the appearance of a new generation of French designers who were autonomous with regard to the dominant polarities of the architecture of the time.[18] Rather distant from each other in their respective styles of articulation, they share a certain elegance — less intellectualised with Lion than with his two partners in London. Intuition orchestrated by observation, to which Lion subscribed, thoroughly defined what could be considered as an architecture of *generosity*. Regarding the work of this "modest citizen," Alexandre Chemetoff maintained in 1992 that "architecture today is necessarily discrete, noble and rigorous, radically normal and at the same time out of place in the domain of dreams and utopias left uncompleted by politics."[19] Lion's architecture rigorously adheres to its internal rules, often achieving this noblesse precisely because it commits itself to a permanent awareness of the human condition.

14. Yves Lion, presentation text, *Grand Prix d'Urbanisme,* 2001.
15. Yves Lion, "Habiter aujourd'hui," *Architecture, mouvement, continuité,* No. 24, September 1981.
16. Yves Lion,"Geoffrey Bawa," *Matières,* vol. 3, 1999, p. 66.
17. Ibid., p. 71.
18. "Developing a lingua franca," *Building Design,* No. 842, 26 June 1987, p. 10.
19. Alexandre Chemetoff, "The Atlantic and the Mediterranean," *Yves Lion* (Barcelona: Gili, 1992), p. 6.

André Lurçat, "Le Mail" housing scheme, Maubeuge, 1954.

Geoffrey Bawa, Piliandala scheme, Sri Lanka.

Chapter One

Modern comfort

On the Saint-Denis Plain, Yves Lion justified the relative over-sizing of the roads designed as a grid of the redevelopment scheme by the *Hippodamos 93* collective by evoking the notion of "comfort." One of the most constant manifestations of the strategy of generosity is precisely that of comfort in everyday spaces, starting with housing. It is not simply a case of increasing mechanically the quantity of living space, but of rearticulating it. Commenting on the project for a cultural centre and festival hall in Vigneux-sur-Seine (1977), he noted that "large housing schemes are saturated by open spaces" and that it is "precisely this which gives them their quality," proposing to "reveal places" whose potential was not exhausted.[20]

However, in a discussion on housing he also affirmed in 1987 that "winning surface" is evidently a necessary struggle, but also that "you don't buy space by the kilo."[21] Without rejecting the importance of an extension of inhabitable volume, notably in social housing, he applies himself to a renewal of comfort features at the scale of the individual apartment. The memory of Moroccan buildings is still pertinent here, since Casablanca in the 1950s was a city with apartments that were better equipped, if not larger than their Parisian counterparts. The typological invention practised by Lion in his public housing follows several paths. It finds its departure point in the Taut housing developments, in the dwellings of Le Corbusier's Unité d'Habitation in Marseilles, for which his admiration is constant but critical, as well as in the apartments of the Haussmann era in Paris, whose flexibility remains exemplary.

20. Yves Lion, "Les salles des fêtes de Vigneux," *Architecture, mouvement, continuité*, No. 41, March 1977, p. 58.
21. Yves Lion, "Loger ou bien réinventer le monde," *L'Architecture d'aujourd'hu[i]*, No. 252, September 1987, p. 21–23 (conversation wi[th] Paul Chemetov, Renée Gai[l]houstet and Jean Nouvel).

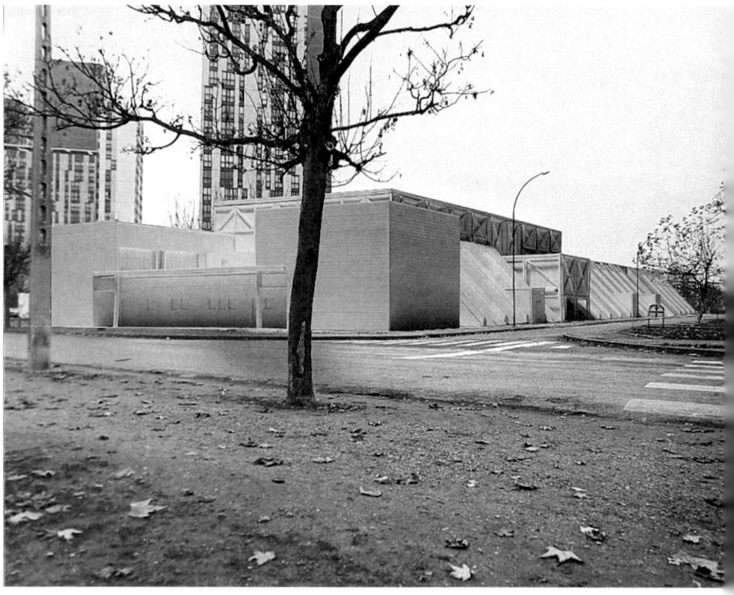

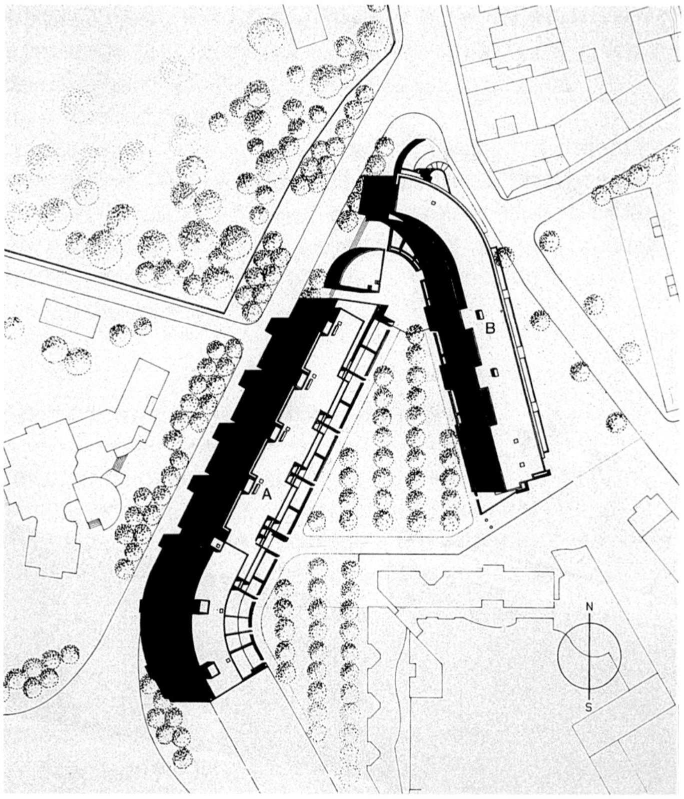

roject for a Cultural
entre and Festival
Hall, Vigneux-sur-Seine,
977, photomontage
of the model.

Housing scheme, Noisy-le-Grand, 1986, massing plan and daily life in a patio.

It was in the 1980s that the office put the accent on the transformation of lived-in space. Thus, in the operation of Noisy-le-Grand (1983–1986), presented by Lion in opposition to the model of the large composition reminiscent of Versailles, then the base of several of Ricardo Bofill's schemes, the choice was left to the inhabitants to modify the size of their apartments as they desired, acquiring an extra room or reducing the surface of their flat by one room, thanks to the provision of flexible areas. The project with François Leclercq of a building of artists' studios (1984–1986) and of an old people's home (1988–1991), built next to each other on the shore of the Bassin de la Villette in Paris, also explored the sculptural potential of the urban façade, seen as an element of habitability and not just a masque facing the city.

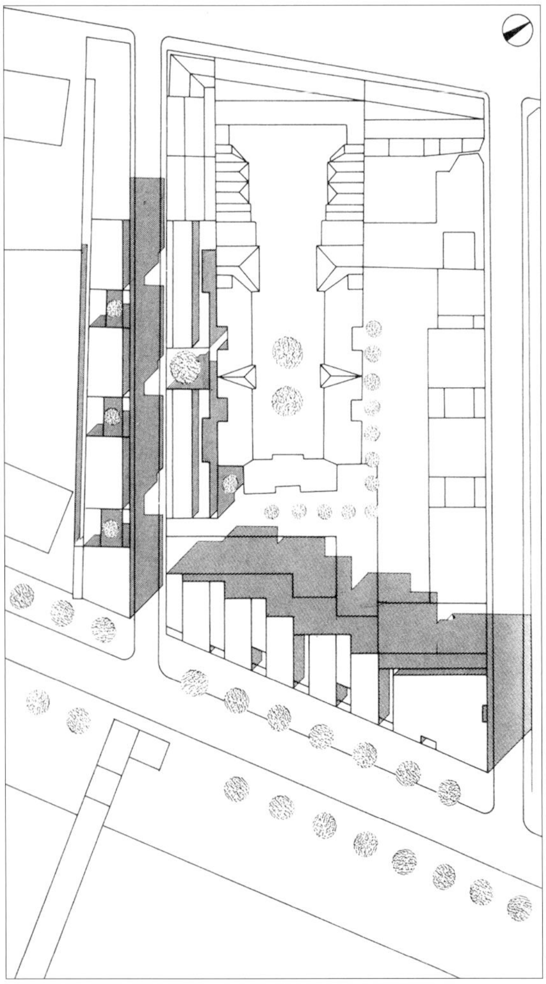

Housing scheme, Quai de Seine, Paris, 19th arrondissement, 1982–1991, massing plan and interior circulation.

Housing scheme, Quai de Seine, Paris, 19th arrondissement, 1982–1991, view across the la Villette canal and corner of the Quai de Seine and the Passage de Flandres.

On the invitation of the "Plan construction," a French public programme engaged in fostering building research and development, Yves Lion and Leclercq drew on these initial experiences between 1984 and 1988 in order to engage in a prospective reflection on housing in the twenty-first century, whose very title, "*Domus demain,*" constituted a conscious provocation. "Inscribing in a perspective of the future" a Latin term which, as they confess, "evokes an idea of permanence," they refused with equal vigour the "reverie on the extension of in-house robotics," the "sociological speculation on the emergence of new practices in housing," and the attempt to "define the long-term evolution of the construction industry."[22] The project derived from a critical analysis of the dwellings of the Unité d'Habitation in Marseilles, certainly "the most beautiful" that Yves Lion had seen "in his life as an amateur of housing," and from the realist acknowledgement that it was difficult to increase floor area and that, at best, it was a question of creating area "illusions."[23] He rejected contemporary building where centres were occupied by "abandoned spaces" and façades "enclosed," advocating the creation of an "active band" on the building's periphery that would accommodate building services and mechanical equipments, a kind of "hyperfaçade" that did "not risk being listed as an historical monument," as Lion wrote, opposing the scheme to the one of the Unités d'Habitation.[24] It is true that the proposed layout contrasted with the "passive" zone at the heart of these.

22. Yves Lion, François Leclercq, "Domus demain, la bande active," *L'Architecture d'aujourd'hui*, No. 252, September 1987, p. 16–20; *Domus demain* (Paris: Plan Construction et habitat, 1988).

23. Yves Lion, interview with Monique Eleb, 7 February 2000 (conducted as part of the film project *Architectures de l'habitation*, La Cinquième Lieurac productions, 2000).

24. Yves Lion, in: *Corbu vu par*... (Paris: Institut français d'architecture/ Liège: Mardaga, 1987), p. 138.

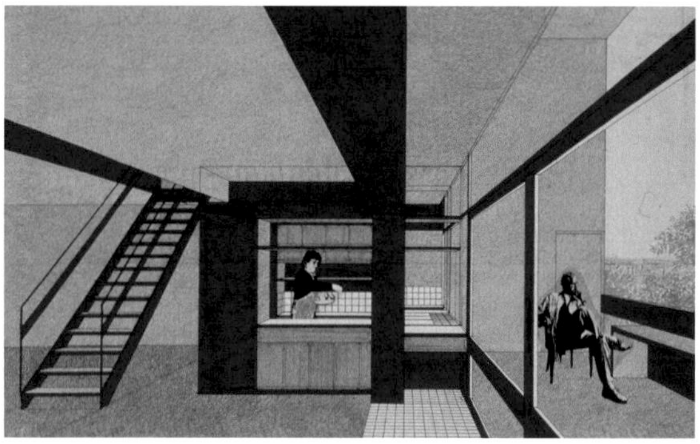

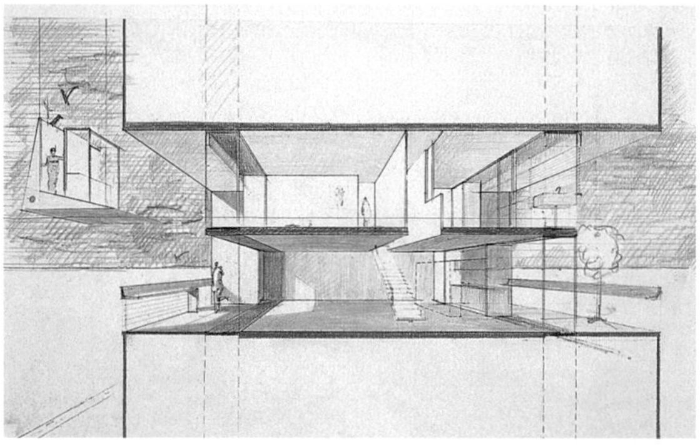

Domus demain project, 1984, «active band», interior view of an apartment, and principle for the assembly of kitchen units.

Domus demain project, 1984, implementation in Berlin (1986), crosssection; assembly diagram; and plan of a twobedroom apartment.

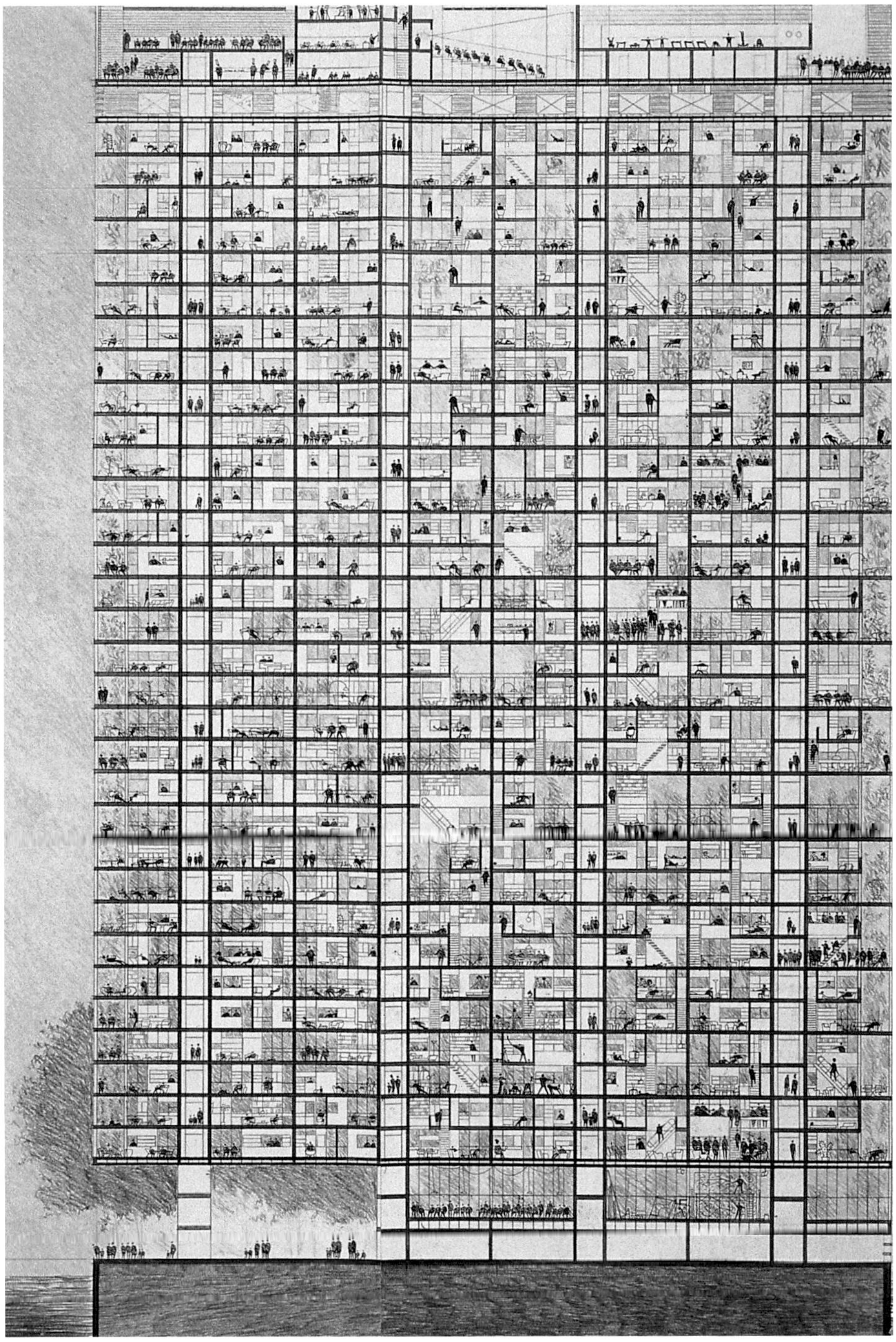

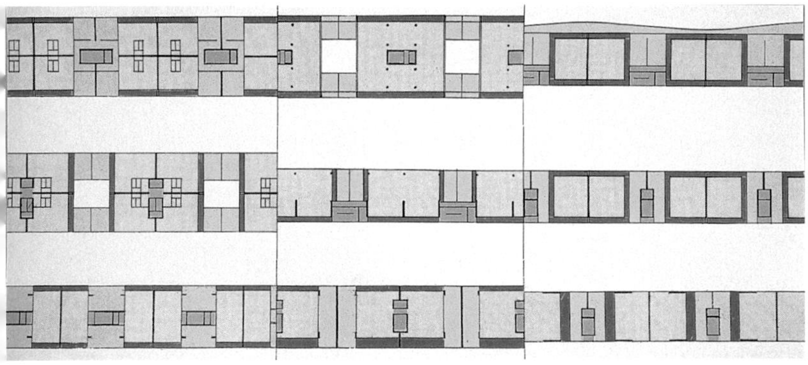

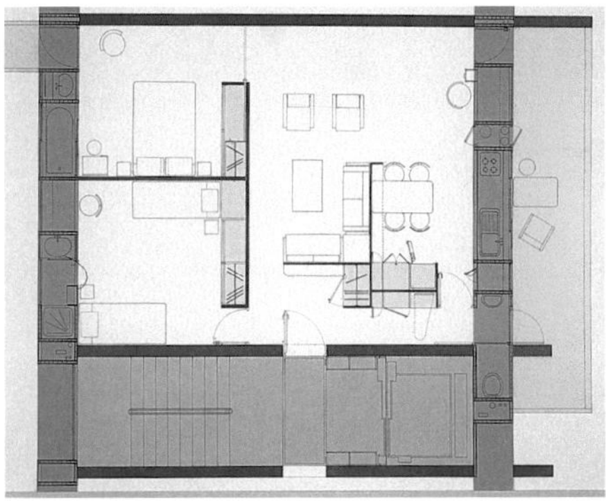

In buildings considerably less deep and therefore built with a more linear footprint, in accordance with this principle, kitchens and bathrooms were to be lit by direct sunlight. The most modern fitting techniques would be carried out with ease on the façades with interchangeable components, the building's frame remaining more traditional. To each bedroom a bathroom was allocated along a façade which served for "supply from outside — light, noise, fluids, energy," and which was re-evaluated as a "dense place at the intersection of the interior and the exterior." On the other hand, the "heart of the dwelling" illustrates its "permanent character." It is this "place of quiet, immobility and peace, of liberty with regard to outdoors, where the very essence of the idea of the home is engraved." This project is a distant echo of research carried out in the Netherlands during the 1960s and 1970s by N. J. Habraken's SAR, whose theory of "supports" tended to differentiate between the permanent structure of buildings and their more flexible and temporary periphery, where an obsolete bathroom, for example, could be replaced by a bedroom.[25] The theoretical principle of "*Domus demain*" was the object of an application to the Berlin situation of 1989, within the framework of the ideas competition "Berlin, Architecture and Utopia." Most importantly, its themes would be deployed in several projects which were built subsequently.

Thus the structures erected in a porous slab in Villejuif (1986–1992) again adopted the principle of putting a bathroom adjacent to each bedroom. Large loggias separated the apartments and were linked to the two-level apartments, permitting an interpretation of Le Corbusier's 1922 Immeuble-villas (freehold maisonettes). This layout was articulated with a design by Alexandre Chemetoff for "living simply" facing a canal and a park.[26] Two buildings built at the same time by Yves Lion in front of the Parc de Bercy stem from a team project carried out with the co-ordinator of the new neighbourhood, Jean-Pierre Buffi, and other architects. In the most constrained financial budget for more economical social housing the element of comfort was constituted by a design encouraging a visual relation to the neighbouring park.[27] The windows and ledges of the rooms at the corners of the buildings were reminiscent of the interior façade of the apartment slabs by Jean Dubuisson in the Maine-Montparnasse scheme, well known to and appreciated by Lion who had lived there for a long time.

25. N. J. Habraken, *De Dragers en de Mensen, het einde van de massawoningbouw* (Amsterdam: Scheltema & Holkema N.V., 1961); in English: *Supports, an Alternative to Mass Housing* (London: the Architectural Press, 1972).

26. "Wohnriegel in Villejuif bei Paris," *Bauwelt*, No. 28–29, 30 June 1993, p. 1522–1525; Jean-Louis Cohen, Monique Eleb, *Paris architecture 1900/2000* (Paris: Norma, 2000), p. 247.

27. Jean-Michel Léger, "Rêver, expérimenter, rectifier/comprendre: les aventures de la 'bande active'/Y. Lion architecte," *Lieux communs*, No. 6, 2002, p. 19–46.

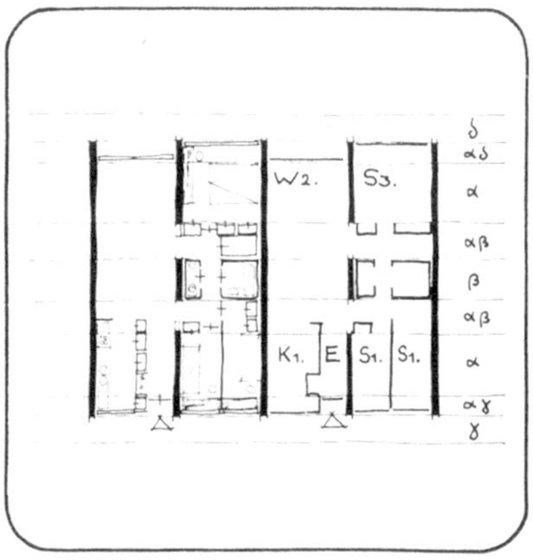

N. J. Habraken, housing plans featuring "supports" and "detachable units."

Social housing scheme, Quartier des Hautes Bruyères, Villejuif, 1986–92, everyday scene on the canal's shore and interior view of a bedroom/bathroom combination.

Another aspect of comfort components was condensed in highly different projects. In the conversion of the Rue Boileau offices (1994–1996), the apartments were largely determined by the demands of future purchasers and negotiated with them. In the case of homes designed for Apollonia in Marseilles and Bordeaux, a step of this kind was not conceivable due to this particular client's expeditious method of selling all apartments within twenty-four hours. It was therefore in the project phase that the diversity of demands made were taken into account, with the creation of dozens of plan variations.

Scheme for 600 housing units, Quartier de la Bastide, Bordeaux, 2002–2008, general plan.

Office building converted into housing, Rue Boileau, Paris, 16th arrondissement, 1996, two exterior views: initial and transformed conditions; three interior views: initial and transformed conditions.

Housing scheme, Quartier de la Joliette, Marseilles, 2004, general plan with Castro-Denissoff architects, a factory converted, and model used for the marketing of the apartments.

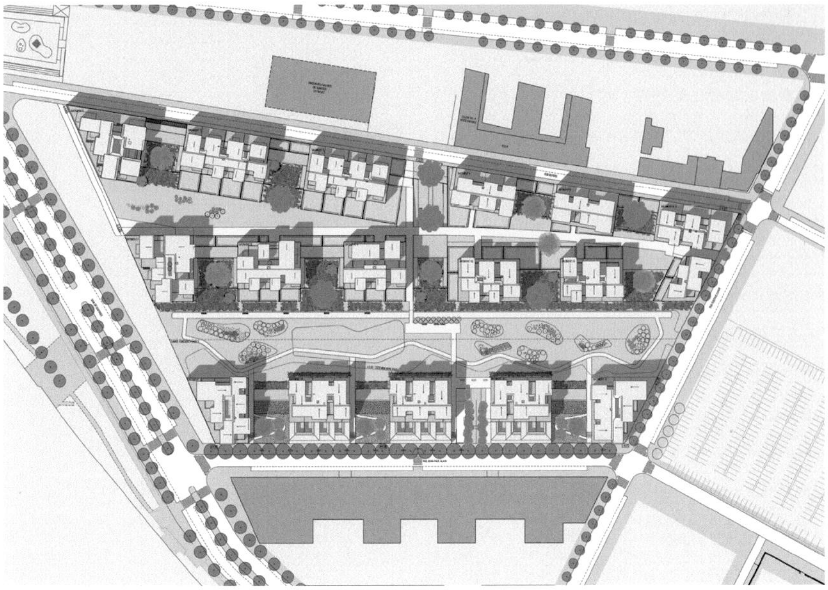

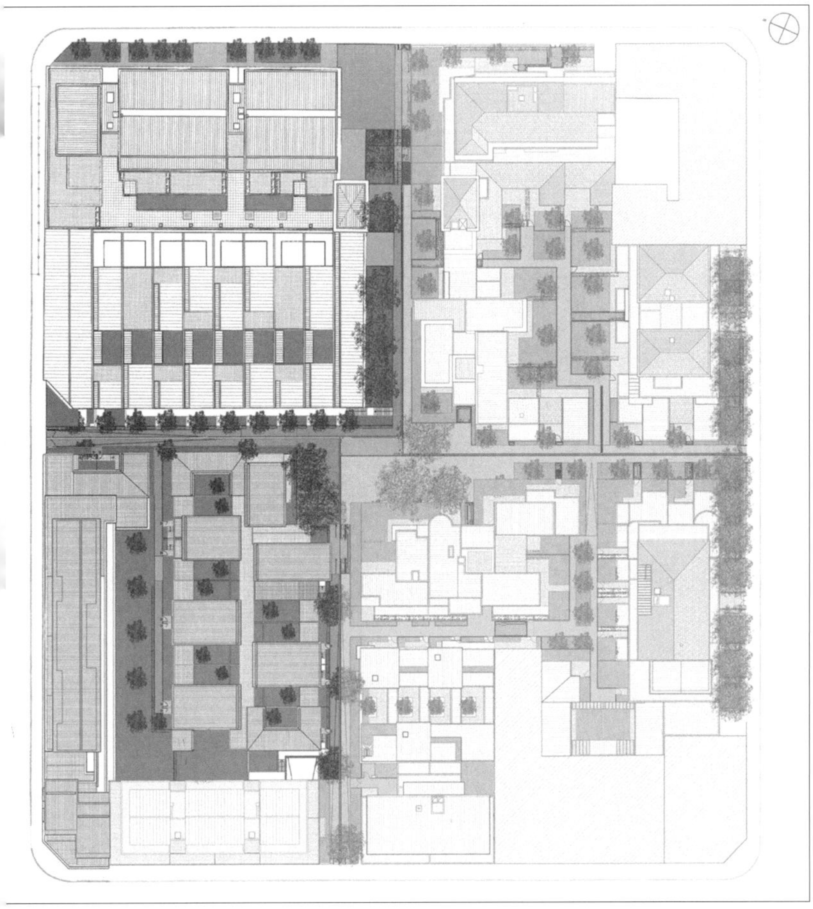

Several housing projects were designed along similar lines. The house built in the Quartier de la Montagne in Tangiers (1990–1991) along the incline visually absorbs through its horizontal windows the view of the distant medina and of the adjacent vernacular urbanisation. The variable permeability between the interior and the exterior and the creation of intermediary spaces, sheltered from the wind and benefiting from sunlight, assured everyday comfort. More delicate due to being conditioned by very strict technical and economical parameters, the prototype designed in 1993–1994 for Maisons Phénix, France's foremost builder of industrialised single-family homes, did not reach the stage of mass-production. Accepting the inevitable pitched roof as an unfortunate given, Yves Lion had nonetheless done his best for this compulsory constructive system — in which the corners of the house were load-bearing and therefore opaque — by installing the living area and the dining room in the more open central area. The exterior "cases" thus permitted a very large variety of arrangements, facilitating future changes by using identical French windows for all openings.[28]

28. Elisabeth Allain-Dupré, "Phénix et ses maisons d'architecte," *Le Moniteur architecture AMC*, No. 41, May 1993, p. 7.

Lion House, Tangiers, 1991, terraces and entrance.

Lion House, Tangiers, 1991, views toward the city.

Study for maisons Phénix, 1992, geometric plan grid, basic layout, two possible evolutions of basic layout, and garden façade.

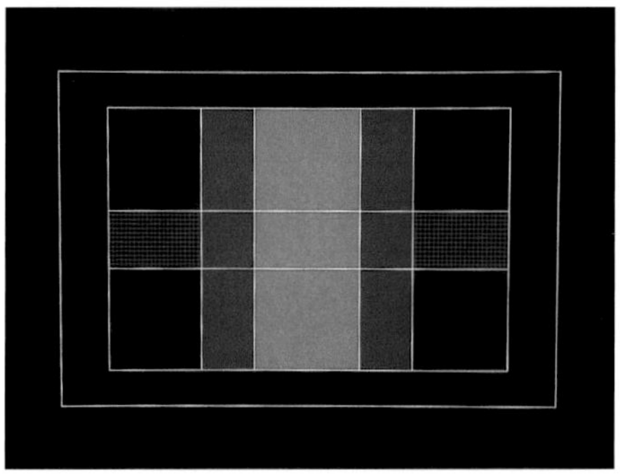

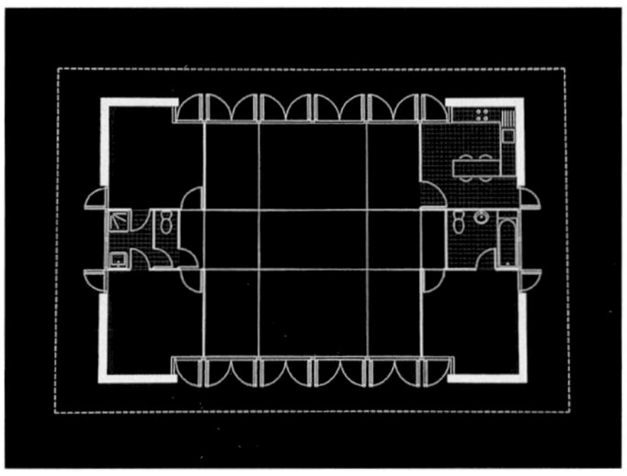

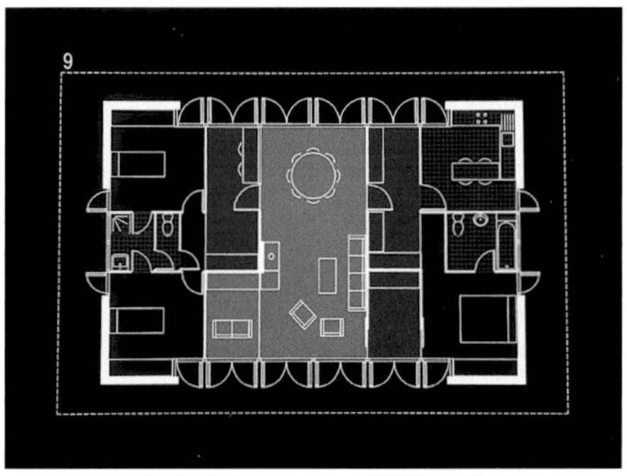

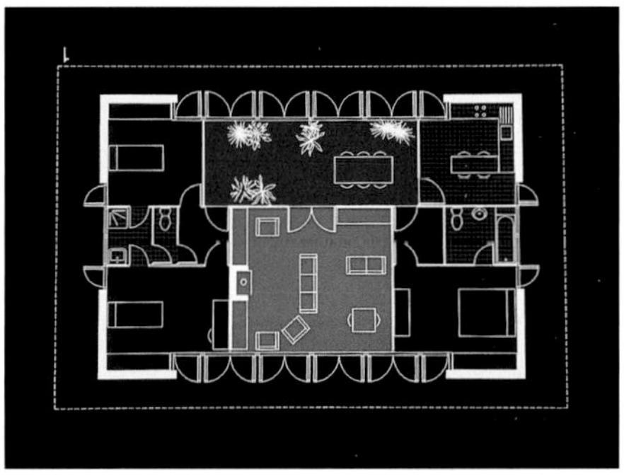

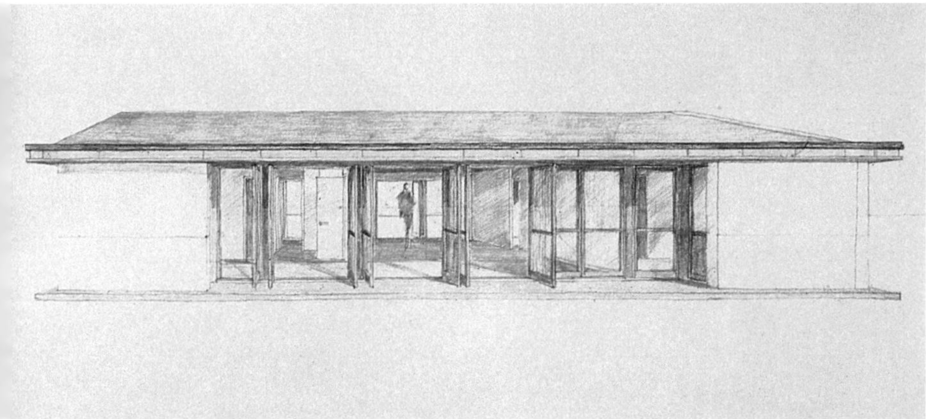

The ease in the comprehension of distribution and in the movement permitted by these projects was not exclusive to domestic designs but can be found in a large measure on the scale of large public development programmes. Comfort therefore primarily becomes a demand for the design of circulation space giving ease to the users' movements. Accessibility is the first quality of Lion's interventions in the galleries of the Grand Louvre, whereas, in the Nantes complex, the generous layout of the great hall and its access to the underground conference room is doubled by the clarity of the circular ambulatories surrounding the opera room.

Convention Centre and Opera, Nantes, 1992, circulations of the Opera auditorium and the Opera seen from the restaurant.

Chapter Two

Déja là

Two strategies of observation characterise Yves Lion's relation to territories in which his development and building projects are inscribed: an analytical procedure and an empathic one. The first is a selective one, picking up from a rational and investigative approach, permitting the updating of networks, structuring features and topographical presences with which the project enters into relation. The second proceeds from a more inclusive approach in which generally overlooked or undervalued minor and aesthetic elements are taken into account in a more restrained strategy of intervention.

Lion's attention to concrete situations derives from a fundamental defiance regarding the abstraction of *Beaux-Arts* projects and the generic character of some Modernist projects. Far from thinking in opposition to the concrete conditions to be met, he underlines that "the context is the enemy of the dogma" and that it is precisely "the starting point of a moral of the housing complex."[29] Moreover, it is in this perspective that he inflects his reading of twentieth-century history, declaring that "modern architecture supplies us with the instruments with which to reflect on the authenticity of a dialogue with the pre-existences."[30] Suggested by Ernesto Nathan Rogers in his editorials of *Casabella-continuità* in the 1950s,[31] the notion of "pre-existences" enlists architecture both in existing spatial configurations and in their history.

Paying great attention to the terrains to which he ventures, Lion is *a priori* prepared to lend them unrecognised qualities; in recollection of the trips to Paris suburbs he organised for his students from Lausanne, he admits that "no site is lost for good." Above all, he is prepared to renounce the idea of using force on the site by wilful intervention and is happy to recommend minimal intervention, or the idea that, in the end, there is perhaps "nothing to do." In this perspective, the work in the city becomes a "craft," one of whose fundamental principles is quite simply "knowing how to erase oneself to a degree" in a given urban situation or "stepping aside" before existing architecture, such as the Louvre.[32] Beginning with the Rochefort competition in 1977, he proposed a strategy of "patient renovation" almost imperceptible on the level of the mass plan for this "part of the town still quite mysterious, hidden."[33]

Following the Law Courts in Draguignan, whose volumes inconspicuously inscribe themselves into the pattern of the quiet Southern Provence town, the vocational school of Saint-Quay-Portrieux in the Côtes d'Armor (1986–1988) illustrated quite literally this approach by refusing a monumental emergence opposed to the lines of the site on the shore of Brittany, already dotted by numerous structures which were both pretentious and mediocre. Held to the terrain like an oil tanker heavily loaded on the sea, the project allowed a calming serenity to rule over a territory ridden with small slate-roofed houses.

Lion's empathic approach presupposes precisely the comprehension and the mobilisation of all existing buildings, whatever their quality or pertinence, to the extent that they are the product of human engagement. As he noted in 1987, it is a case of "taking charge of the context, the whole context, not just of what seems right for you and corresponds to your culture, but that which is built, what the modern world has produced, at a great effort, but has produced while others did not have this opportunity."[34]

29. Yves Lion, "À propos d'urbanisme," 1990.
30. Yves Lion, "L'architecte comme producteur," interview with Pierre-Alain Croset, in: *Yves Lion*, 1992, p. 12.
31. Ernesto N. Rogers, *Editoriali di architettura* (Turin: Einaudi, 1968), p. 123.
32. Yves Lion, "Projets parisiens," p. 15, 22 and 23.
33. Yves Lion, Daniel Tajan, "Concours de Rochefort," *Architecture, mouvement, continuité*, No. 42, June 1977, p. 64.
34. Yves Lion, letter to Ricky Burdett, Gallery 9H, 1987.

Town planning competitio Rochefort-sur-Mer, 1978, general plan.

Vocational school, Saint-Quay-Portrieux, Brittany, 1989, view from the air and view of the restauran

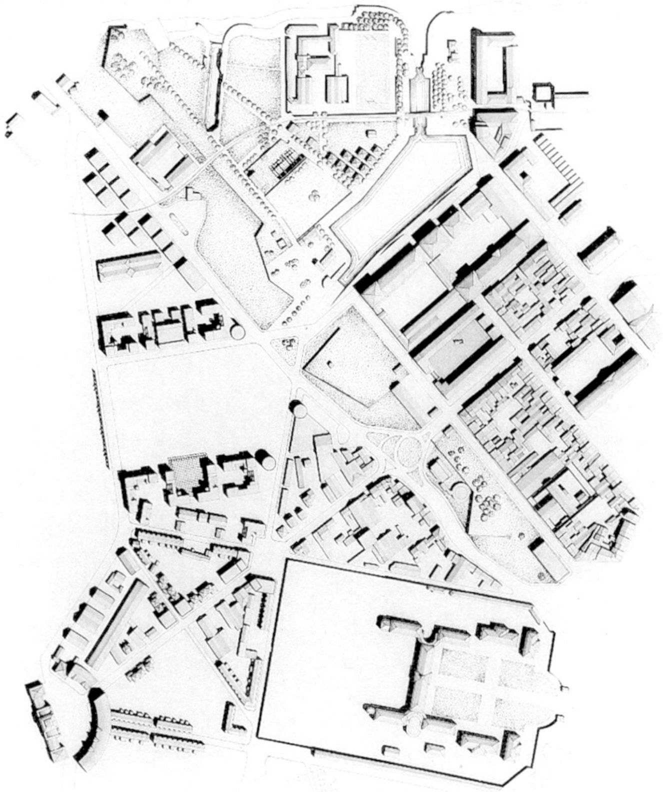

On the scale of the single building, Yves Lion never fails to observe projects neglected by official architectural history, conscious of the fact that, in analogy with Hollywood film productions, there "existed all over the world a whole range of B series buildings that had contributed to the making of modern towns."[35] Thus, alongside the buildings consecrated to the masters of the "Modern Movement," Lion's imaginary museum incorporates buildings from the 1930s in North Africa or the Middle East, factories and villas in suburbs of Paris and a sprawling corpus of "spontaneous" constructions and facilities on all continents. And when he demands "a radically banal practice,"[36] he is doubtlessly referring to the masters of these unrecognised or anonymous works rather than to the prominent "A series" ones.

This approach worked best in the landscapes for which he had the longest affinity; this led him to rethink his initial perceptions. When building his house in Tangiers, he was "struck" by the "incredible ability" of the newly urbanised rural people "to appropriate the sites through the efficiency of the encounter of Berber and Arab culture and also that of Europe to some extent when it is a question of building the texture of a city. Where the entire Modern movement has failed, these people living in the suburbs manage to use timeless impulses to domesticate the gradient." In order to build, he therefore looked to a quarter he considered to be a "lesson for planners," drawing on "modest capitals, repatriated by workers from Europe who build on small plots, barely equipped with amenities, buildings that stick to the slightest difference in level and which find their economic balance between the volume and height permitted by the most economical structural system."[37]

In 1991 he was asked by the local State authorities in Tangiers to design the redevelopment of the Grand Socco Square, the main gate to the city's market; the authorities were concerned with emphasizing the identity of a city subjected to strong demographical and speculative pressures. Proposing the destruction of the shacks on the location, he pursued the sequence of urban spaces dominating the medina in order to create a forum lined with arcades in the middle of which the Sidi Bouabid Mosque was to find its monumental role, similar to that of the Pêcherie Mosque on Government Square in Algiers, allowing for the visual rediscovery of the Straits of Gibraltar in the distance.

In contrast to this reconciliation with urban voids, the 1994 project for the reconstruction of the bazaar quarter in Beirut suggested a redevelopment of the solids, restoring its density to a place which before the civil war was shared by all social and religious groups of the Lebanese capital. The project operated on two levels: above a car park with an implacably orthogonal geometry, and a texture representing the complexity of the ancient quarter one storey above street level, without an artificially modern corset being imposed upon it. The old Rue de Trablous crossed it, linked to the shops by way of stairways.[38] It was a process that was left to unfold without the accent being put on the excellence of projects to come; the principle of assembly was planned to integrate even the buildings of "C series."

35. Yves Lion, presentation text, *Grand prix d'urbanisme*, 2001.
36. Yves Lion, "Projets parisiens," p. 16.
37. Yves Lion, presentation text, *Grand prix d'urbanisme*, 2001.
38. "Schneller Wiederaufbau?," *Werk, Bauen + Wohnen*, November 1994, p. 43.

Study for the redevelopment of the Grand Socco square, Tangiers, 1991, photomontage.

Competition for the reconstruction of the bazaar quarter, Beirut, 1994, view of a street.

SOUK AL JAMIL

The French Embassy in Beirut (1997–2002) is situated not far from the Résidence des Pins in the south of the city. It was added to the pleasant "pre-existences" that were the buildings surrounded by porticoes built by the elegant architects Jean-Charles Moreux and André Leconte. Opening its wings onto the grounds occupied by the French administration and towards the mountains in the distance, it constitutes the tip of a large block turned towards the centre to which the antique Rue de Damas led. Its solid stone volumes echo the walls of the Phoenicians and Romans, the Ottoman houses and the buildings of the French Mandate, draped in Ramleh stone on the exterior and coiled around a quiet courtyard. In its relationship to the vicinity it can be compared to Lion's notations on Bawa, who "built his house and garden on the side of a hill. [...] As architect and landscaper, he does not see much distinction between the interior and exterior, nor does his country. [...] With this architect one could say that the objective is the pathway."[39]

39. Yves Lion, "Geoffrey Bawa," p. 66.

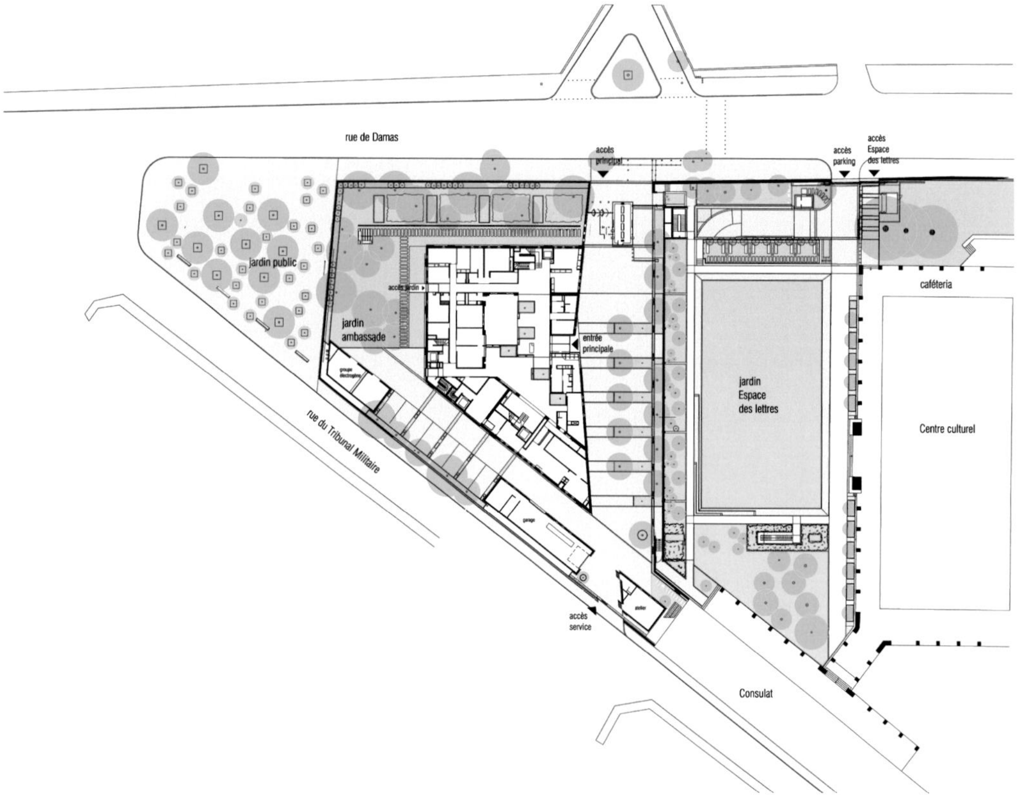

This spread:
French Embassy, Beirut, 2003, plan and exterior view.

Next spread:
French Embassy, Beirut, 2003, exterior view at dusk.

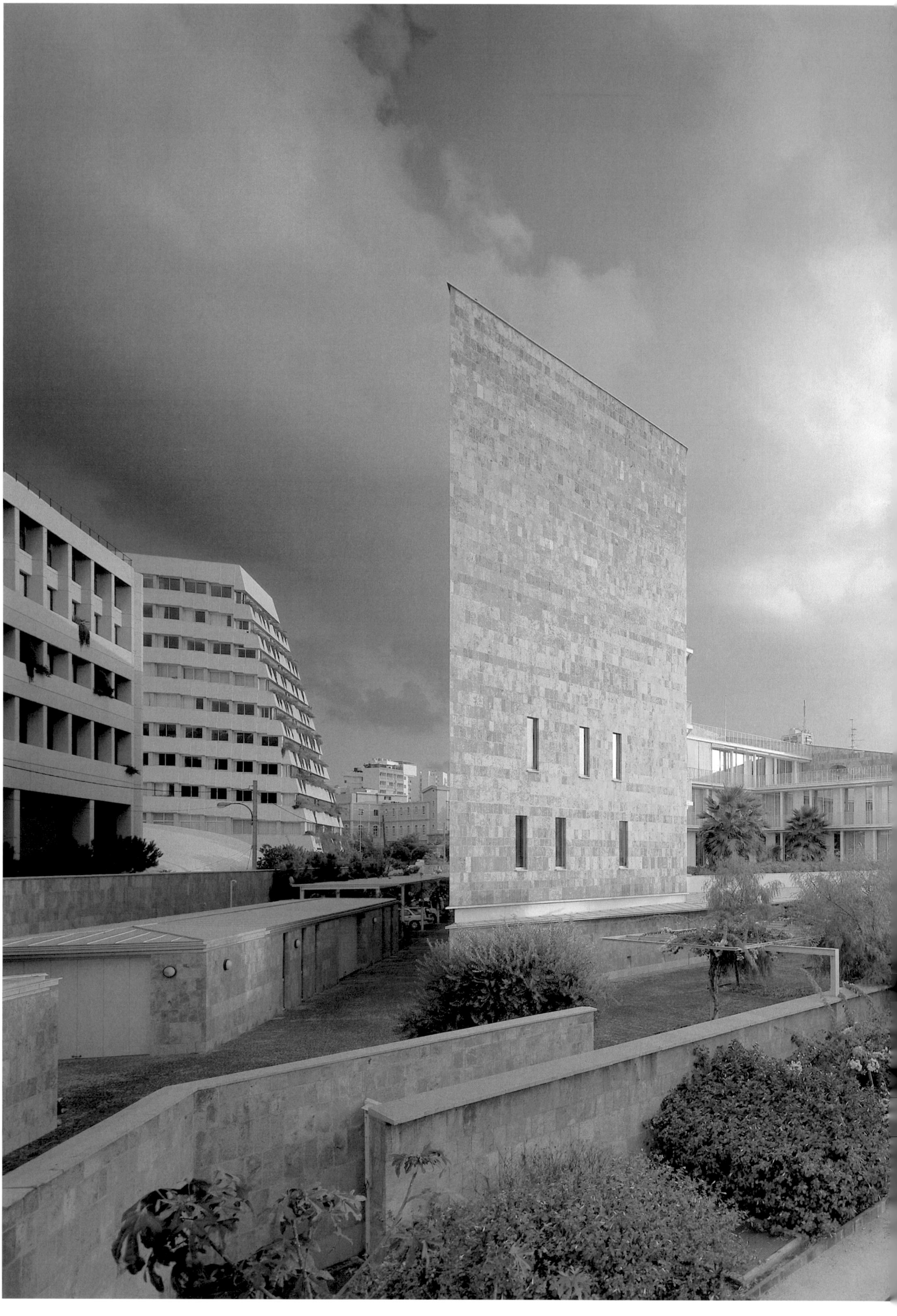

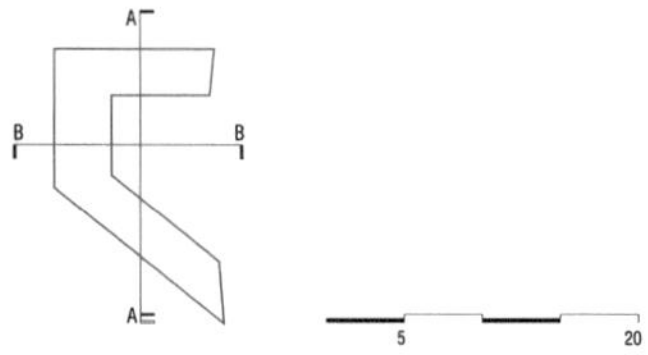

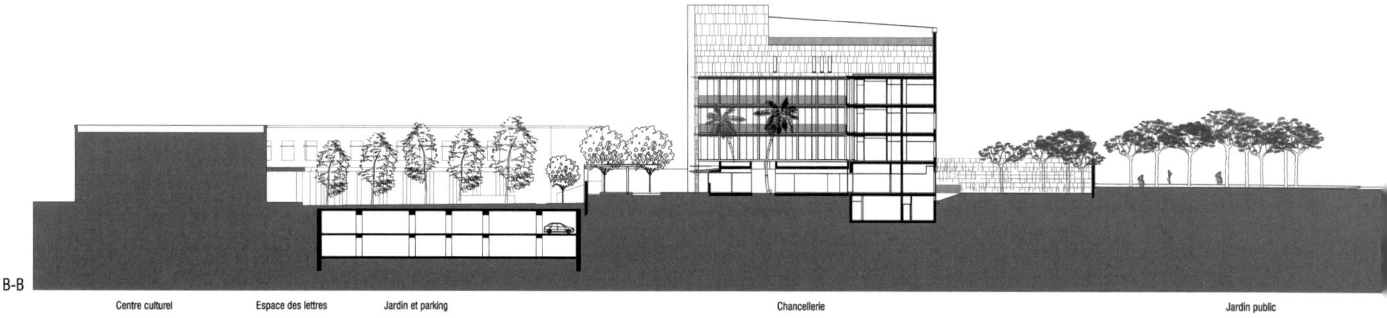

French Embassy, Beirut, 2003, cross sections, view with surrounding townscape, view with the gardens, and protective walls.

French Embassy, Beirut, 2003, two views of the entrance hall and patio, typical office, and offices of the chancellor.

Chapter Three

Homage to architecture, or being "completely against" it...

Yves Lion's attention to "B series" in architectural history does not exhaust his intimate relationship with the built-up landscape. One significant part of his production lies in conversions or extensions which may pose the problems of interpreting existing buildings and of the distance one assumes to them. These interventions dealing with outstanding buildings inscribed in architectural history, or with those at least recognisable as oeuvres, presuppose a critical complicity that was sometimes delicate to assume.

In the project for the redesign of the Porte de la Villette in Paris, the old abattoirs by Henri Colboc were squeezed in a kind of mortal grip, since the scheme proposed to transform the giant building into an interior structure surrounded by new constructions. This extreme form was exceptional; from the mid-1980s the office pursued programmes of extension, redevelopment or conversion, for the greater part with understanding and ambitious clients.

On the same theme, two unsuccessful competition entries for the extension of the Rodin Museum (1988) and the restructuring of the Collège de France (1993), both under the careful custody of the Administration of Historical Monuments, provided only sketchy visions of what might have been if they had been built. In the former case, new galleries were created beneath the museum's garden, thus preserving above ground the classical appearance of the Hôtel Biron. Only the edges of its wings would have been perceived from the buried main floor. In the latter case, the visual contact with the complex by Jean-François Chalgrin was limited to the exterior and the addition of a vertical library built in accordance with the *cour d'honneur* under which a large amphitheatre was created, the task of representing the institution being achieved "beneath the building."[40]

40. Yves Lion, "Projets parisiens," p. 22.

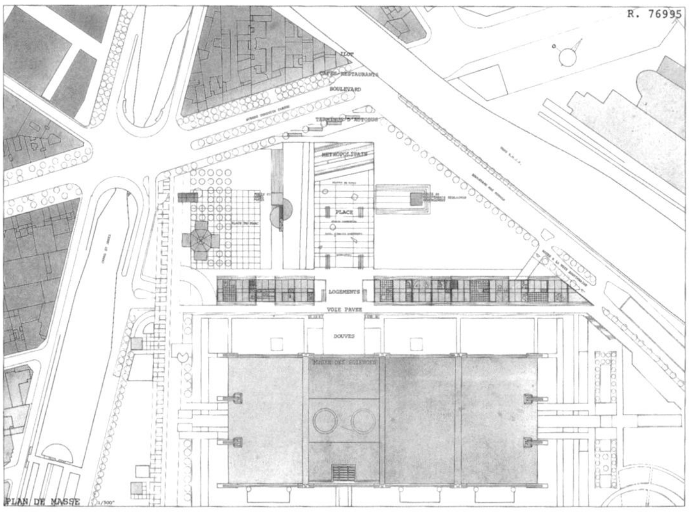

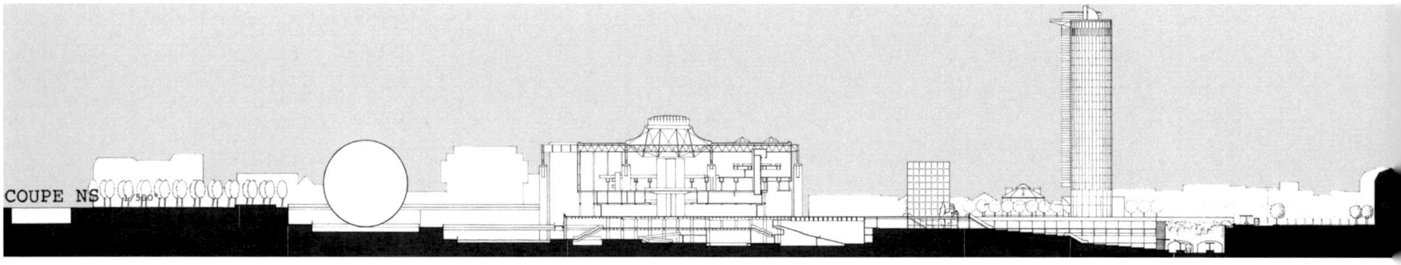

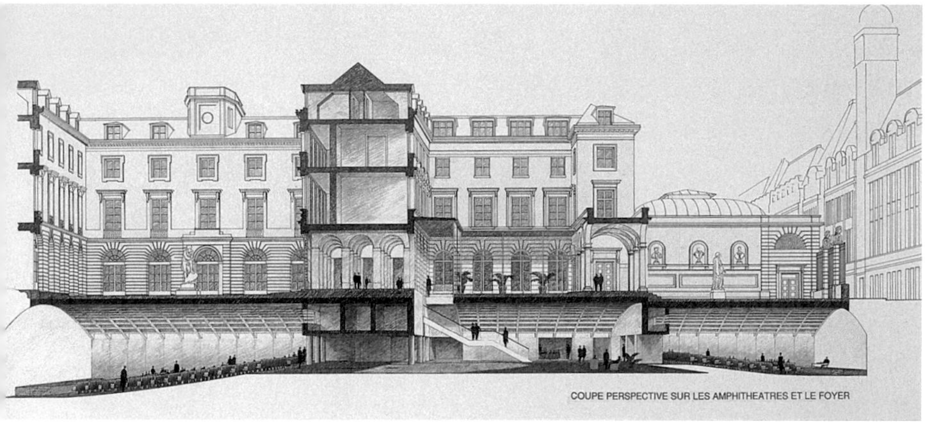

COUPE PERSPECTIVE SUR LES AMPHITHEATRES ET LE FOYER

Competition for the extension of the Rodin Museum, Paris, 7th arrondissement, 1988, view of the main exhibition galleries.

:ompetition for housing nd a hotel in front of ıe la Villette science ıuseum, Paris, 19th rrondissement, 1984, lan and longitudinal ection on the entire site.

Competition for the restructuring of the Collège de France, Paris, 5th arrondissement, 1993, section on the courtyard, the underground auditoria, and view toward the library.

Two other extensions built at an interval of around a decade sheltered museum programmes; both could not fail to make the staging of architecture a component of the experience the public would go through during the visit. The Blérancourt Château in the Aisne already had a troubled history when the question of its enlargement was raised. Built by Salomon de Brosse in the early seventeenth century it was seriously disfigured when the American heiress Ann Morgan decided in 1916 to establish a base for United States military and sanitary aid to wartime France. The creation after the armistice of a Museum of Franco-American Cooperation led to an initial enlargement in the form of two pavilions transposing de Brosse's composition in a neoclassical style not free of rigidity. It was doubly against this collage that the extension was built in 1987–1989: in *opposition* to it, as well as *completely against it*, that is in intimate contact with it, according to a famous pun by playwright Sacha Guitry.[41] Built onto the recent pavilions to which new spans were added, it distanced itself at the same time from them, thereby enhancing the ensemble. By a sort of inversion, the laconism of the extension's spaces did not come across as an addition but, instead, as providing a frame of reference that magnified the adjacent château as though it were its support. The use of a steel skeleton to which the stone cladding was attached permitted the creation of horizontal windows serving as joints between the historic base and the new wall, an interval between the walls assuring the same effect vertically, not failing to evoke the fissure of light separating the 1953 Yale University Art Gallery by Louis I. Kahn in New Haven from the neo-gothic envelope of the old museum. Inside, the reorganised vertical circulation, adjacent to a newly created wall, permitted to overcome the limits of the pavilions in order to put up longer sequences of paintings under a light that was serene and homogenous.[42]

41. A famous reply by Sacha Guitry, French actor and dramaturge (1885–1957), to the question "Are you for or against women?" was: "I am against, completely against …"

42. Surprised by the success of this extension of an "obscure" country museum, the journal *Progressive Architecture* praised it: Barbara Shortt, "Kudos for an American Museum in France," *Progressive Architecture*, No. 8, August 1990, p. 31–32.

This spread:
Museum of Franco-American Cooperation, Blérancourt, 1989, exterior view with one of the original pavilions, the pastiche and the new wing.

Next spread:
Museum of Franco-American Cooperation, Blérancourt, 1989, frontal view with the castle's plinth, the 1930s pastiche and the museum's new wing.

Museum of Franco-American Cooperation, Blérancourt, 1989, two views of the exhibition galleries and corner view of a gallery.

The creation by the City of Paris of a European House of Photography in the Hôtel Hénaut de Cantobre (1990–1996) was the occasion for a larger and more complex extension which intertwines with a complex building and its urban situation on the southern fringe of the historic Marais district. The undertaking was the riskiest project of the entire cultural regaining of this urban quarter where Roland Simounet built the Picasso Museum, since the modifications were perfectly visible from the street and were not hidden in an interior courtyard.[43] Like in Blérancourt, the restrained and linear addition avoided stealing the show from the historic building on Rue François Miron to which it was joined by way of a glass link, to name another similarity. On the ground floor a stone wall and a covered zinc entranceway enveloped the garden and connected the ensemble to the Rue de Fourcy. Transformed into galleries, the spaces of the original Hôtel particulier were kept in their original proportions while the basement accommodated new facilities, encased in wooden panelling, such as the auditorium and the library to which a narrow band of light gave partial natural lighting.

43. Jean-Paul Robert is vehement in his stance against the conversion of the hôtel: "Le syndrome d patrimoine," *L'Architectu d'aujourd'hui*, No. 304, April 1996, p. 43.

This spread:
Extension of the Hôtel Hénault de Cantobre, Paris, 4th arrondissement, 1788, European House of Photography, 1996, entrance gallery and exterior view of the connection.

Next spread:
Extension of the Hôtel Hénault de Cantobre, Paris, 4th arrondissement, 1788, European House of Photography, Paris, 1996, a friendly cohabitation.

LA PHOTOGRAPHIE

Extension of the Hôtel Hénault de Cantobre, Paris, 4th arrondissement, 1788, European House of Photography, Paris, 1996, exhibition galleries in the new wing (left); exhibition galleries in the former mansion and the information desk (opposite).

:xtension of the Hôtel
lénault de Cantobre,
'aris, 4th arrondisse-
nent, 1788, European
louse of Photography,
'aris, 1996, the listed
istoric stairs and exhibi-
ion galleries on the upper
oor (opposite); two views
f the library (right).

Any kind of extension to the Louvre was clearly out of the question, the controversy over the addition of I. M. Pei's glass pyramid on its grounds barely having calmed down and its lengthy construction work still ahead. Yves Lion participated in vain in the consultations for the redevelopment of the Denon pavilion (1993), that of the French painting rooms (1994) and the installation of the Louvre School in the Flore Wing (1994). But in 1996–1998 he completed the remodelling of the Percier & Fontaine and Duchâtel rooms with Alan Levitt and in 1994–1999 the creation of the Porte des Lions entrance and the refurbishing of the Spanish and Italian painting rooms. The principles established in Blérancourt were applied this time to the interior configuration of the walls and to the interior sequences. The new well-lit and rational spaces enhanced the historical walls and ceilings and provided visual shortcuts between rooms as well as resting places. They thus contributed to the discovery of the initial solutions of Percier & Fontaine and Hector Le Fuel. The devices imagined in 1999 for the Salle des États were more radical, and notably the system of suspended screens that was conceived to frame the Mona Lisa, did not convince the jury of the 1999 competition. On the other hand, the stairway of the Porte des Lions and its zigzag walls in white stone introduced a dynamic and restrained rupture to this sensitive precinct.

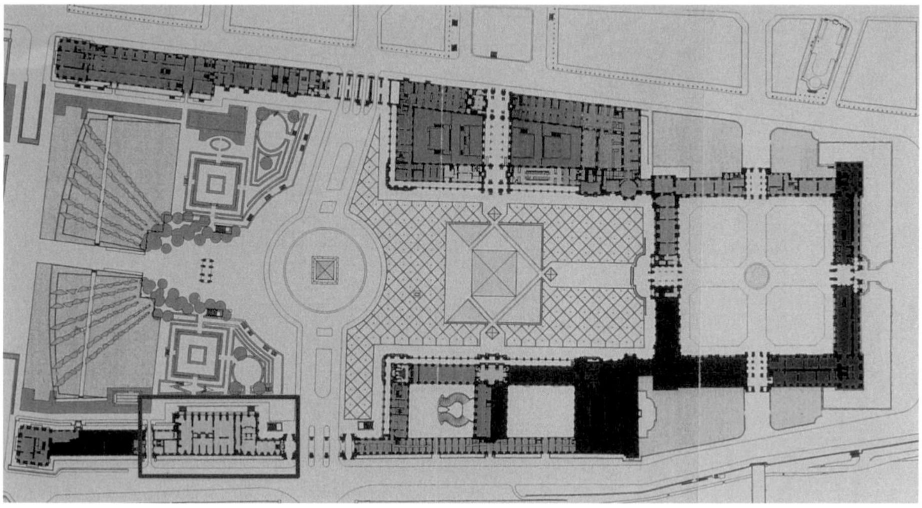

Musée du Louvre, Porte des Lions entrance, Paris, 1st arrondissement, 1999, general plan with area of intervention; the information desk and stairs to the galleries; the new entrance seen from the Seine embankment; and the information desk at the Porte des Lions.

Musée du Louvre, Italian and Spanish galleries, Paris, 1st arrondissement, 1999, Goya gallery and view from the Goya gallery toward the Tuileries gardens.

Musée du Louvre, Italian and Spanish galleries, Paris, 1st arrondissement 1999, light intervention in the gallery built by Percier & Fontaine and two other views of the suite of galleries.

Musée du Louvre,
Prints and drawings
gallery, Paris, 1st
arrondissement, 2001.

The attention to an existing constellation was also visible in the solution for the transformation of offices into apartments in the Rue Boileau. The features conceived by Urbain Cassan, the architect of the initial project from 1958, and of certain other Parisian buildings of the same modern academic vein, were not negated. The exterior signs of the new domestic purpose were provided by wooden shutters. The addition of continuous linear balconies on four levels did not erase the vertical double-frame of Cassan, which remained visible in a composition clearly revealing the historical sequence experienced by the building over four decades.

Office building converted into housing, Rue Boileau, Paris, 1996, architectural superimposition.

Chapter Four

Paris vu par'' Lion

Discovering Paris after arriving from Casablanca in the 1960s was incontestably a shock. The black walls of the urban scenery of "New Wave" films, cut with the luminous façades left behind in Africa and the lack of comfort in the old buildings came as a shock. At the same time urban renewal took over the outer quarters, with large housing schemes being built in the suburbs. Only a few initiatives from the architectural practices Atelier de Montrouge or Atelier d'Urbanisme et d'Architecture (AUA) suggested lasting alternatives to the large-scale production of projects reflecting the deathly alliance of superficial Modernism and Beaux-Art academicism prevalent at the time.

Lion's first exercises took him to the working-class suburbs, starting with Vigneux, a municipality that long since welcomed the projects of the AUA, but also to inner-Paris areas such as La Roquette or La Villette. Throughout these varied quarters, Yves Lion's projects constituted an archipelago, reminiscent of sketches by Chabrol, Rouch, Douchet, Rohmer, Pollet and Godard in the film *Paris vu par* (Six in Paris) of 1965. His project for the Les Halles competition (1979) was a long building of 1,500 apartments stretching from the Saint-Eustache Church and the Boulevard de Sébastopol, expressing, as he recalled, "the idea that one must make the most of the centre of Paris, now ridden of its warehouses, functions and existing buildings in order to welcome dwellers there, and so that the Châtelet (in a way the centre of the Paris region) may be able to accommodate a large quarter of apartments in the heart of the capital." Paradoxically, this project meant to reclaim "more attention" for the centre, and to break off from the "insolent isolation" of the suburbs, but by introducing "the very suburban order to the heart of the city." Lion could not rest since realising "the sad evolution of this city which has, in three decades, lost its familiar character, become increasingly richer, insolent and chic but still has the most beautiful urban structure that exists."[44]

His first completed projects suggested a play with Parisian textures, from urban planning regulations to the tectonic character of major and minor works of architecture; even in Paris he attached great importance to observing the "B Series." But in 1992 he noted that "the research of typological orthodoxy regarding the constitution of texture, notably in Paris, is an ineffective research that has revealed nothing" and he did not think that it had "succeeded in developing the street." "Too little theory has been produced on the City of Paris" and "regulations ended up being badly interpreted, such as the attempt at homogeneity, known as Neo-Hausmannism."[45] Near the Bassin de la Villette, on the Quai de la Seine, it was in opposition to this strictly conceived Neo-Hausmannism that the volumes of a building of artist studios and the loggias of apartments for the elderly were created, rejecting imitation and practising a sculptural game that strongly singularised them. In a quarter almost entirely conserved in its nineteenth-century condition, the building housing Lion's office on Rue Didot practised another type of composition, accepting the area's strict building code, from which the building's volume with a large zinc roof derived, but with an inversed the treatment of the façade. The bow window facing onto the street brought to Paris a device experimented with in Blérancourt. The partly opaque marble volume protected the intimacy of the offices, marked a clear break in the street frontage line.

44. Yves Lion, presentation text, *Grand prix d'urbanisme*, 2001.
45. Yves Lion, "Comment faire la ville? Entretien avec Yves Lion," p. 123–124.

International competition for the Les Halles area, Paris, 1979, general plan

Atelier d'architecture, Rue Didot, Paris, 14th arrondissement, 1989, view from the interior of the block.

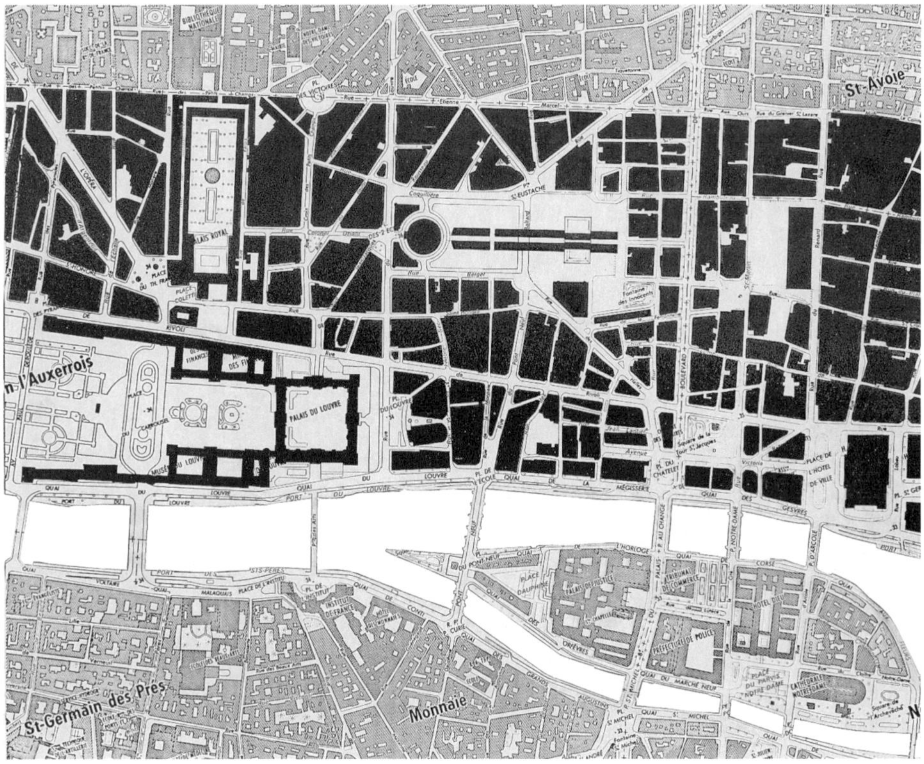
St-Avoie
St-Germain des Pres
Monnaie

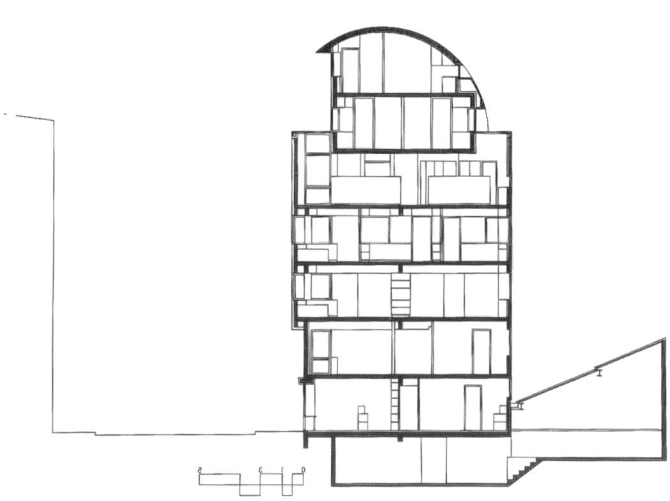

Lion's intervention as a designer for the *Paris des Faubourgs* exhibition, curated by Jacques Lucan in the Pavillon de l'Arsenal (1996), revealed to him "the extent to which the building plot pattern, even the forgotten pattern, was able to serve as starting point for the urban project."[46] These initial projects were guided by this real-estate subdivision that the redevelopment zones (ZAC) had abolished only to recreate it with varied subtlety. The most recent projects participated in a complex game for which the plot pattern was a mere parameter in the composition with the alignments and the surrounding volumes. The apartments at Rue Francœur (1997–1999) are articulated to the premises of the Institut de Formation et d'Enseignement pour les Métiers de l'Image et du Son (FEMIS, formerly known under the name IDHEC), located in the former Pathé Studios still haunted by the ghosts of Jean Renoir and Marcel Carné; the intention of this articulation is to create a Parisian landscape without any rhetoric, at peace in its rapports with the existing city. The building stretched along a new street in the Alésia-Montsouris redevelopment zone (1997–2001) continues this harmonising impulse, establishing a tactile link to the gables of the old structures surrounding it through the treatment of its plinth. It took up the creative plot structure of this new quarter in the freer composition of its superstructure. On a terrain that is delicate due to its unevenness, the Pole for Oriental Languages and Civilisations project (2004) responds on the one hand to the discontinued order of most of the quarter's frontlines and, on the other, to the reticulated geometry of the extension of Le Corbusier's Salvation Army Cité de Refuge, on which the new building will lean by means of delicate metallic beams. The use of bricks connects the proposed complex both to neighbouring mid-twentieth century low-cost housing and to the crate framing this classic of Modern architecture.

46. Yves Lion, presentation text, *Grand prix d'urbanisme*, 2001.

FEMIS Film school and social housing, Rue Francœur, Paris, 18th arrondissement, 2001, general plan.

FEMIS Film school in the former Pathé cinema studios, Paris, 18th arrondissement, 1999, entrance.

FEMIS Film school and social housing, Rue Francœur, Paris, 18th arrondissement, 2001, view of the block's interior.

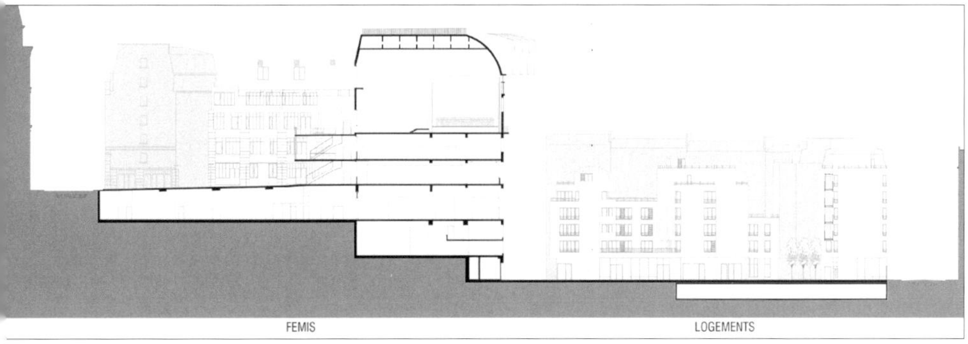

ˆEMIS Film school
.nd social housing, Rue
ˆrancœur, Paris, 18th
arrondissement, 1999,
ˆiew from the block's core
vith the school and the
.partments.

ˆEMIS Film school
ınd social housing, Rue
ˆrancœur, Paris, 18th
.rrondissement, 1997,
ross-section of the two
rogrammes.

ˆocial housing in the
Alésia-Montsouris
eighbourhood, Paris,
.4th arrondissement,
ˆ001, street view.

A larger project implemented above the Quai Henri IV on the grounds of the historic Schomberg Barracks (1994–1999) was located in the more open landscape of the Seine Embankment, in spite of the fence that enclosed it. This project's parameters were defined by the preservation of the building bulk of the metal and brick structures and by the strong presence of the neighbouring prefecture offices of Albert Laprade on Boulevard Morland. A critical contextualism led to the "levelling" of the restored buildings, whose raised height was made clearly visible, and to the use of this method on the new buildings with the theme of Laprade's superstructure decoration. The porosity of the row of buildings along the quay and their repetition nevertheless had nothing of the rigidity encountered further upstream on the Seine, most notably with the apartment buildings standing to attention in an almost military manner around the François Mitterrand Library.

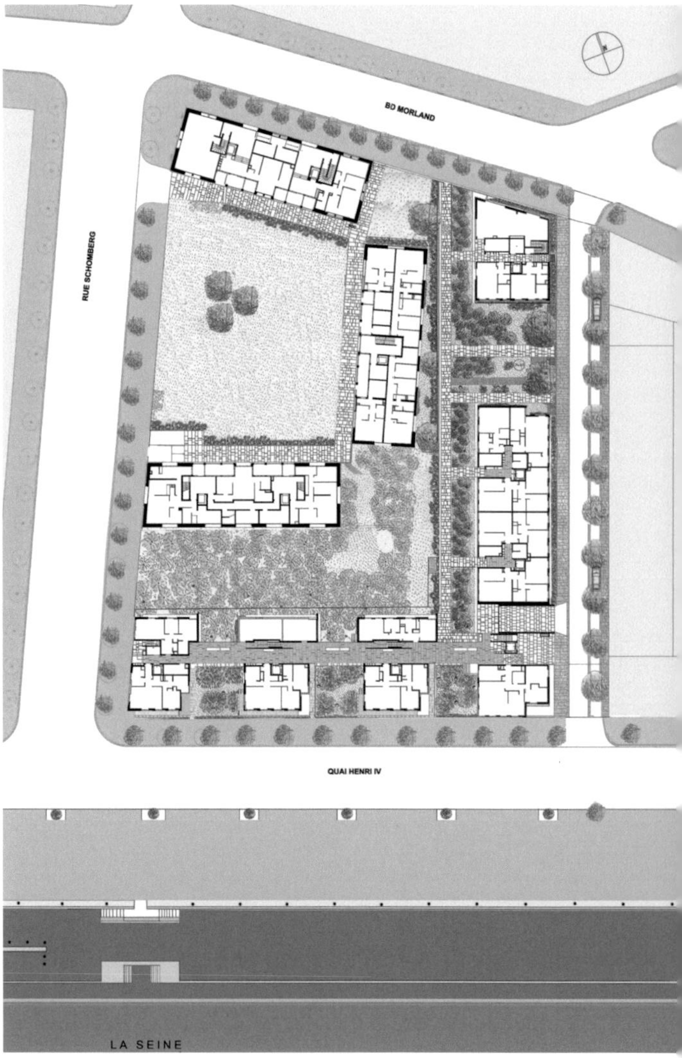

-lousing scheme for the
City of Paris and for
he Republican Guards,
Quartier Schomberg,
Quai Henri IV, Paris, 4th
arrondissement, 1998–
1999, general plan, view
oward the Seine and view
across the Seine.

Social housing in the preserved part of the Schomberg barracks, Paris, 4th arrondissement, 1999, views from the boulevard Sully Morland.

Housing scheme for the Republican Guards, Quartier Schomberg, quai Henri IV, Paris, 4th arrondissement, 1998, view toward the Saint-Louis island and an apartment's terrace.

In the image of the fourteenth arrondissement where he resides, the Paris of Yves Lion is stretched out between the narrow grid of the faubourgs and the valley cut by the Boulevard Périphérique, Paris's circular motorway. The experience of a town-planning consultation in which he played the role of mediator between the inhabitants and the city in the quarter of the Rue des Thermopyles (1997–2000) made him aware of the density of the territories bordering on Paris, both in human and architectural terms.[47] But the question of the Boulevard Périphérique, built between 1957 and 1973, not merely as a technical project dealing with mobility, but also as landscape on an urban scale, had not ceased to preoccupy him since 1990.[48] He thus carried out two studies on the Porte d'Italie and the Porte de Saint-Cloud, endeavouring to "prove that it was possible to pass from the centre to the periphery without being aware of it" and without the notion of a "nostalgic and retrograde" gate before the City of Paris. His approach to the question was — once more — founded on a "return to geography," and thus to considering "the waterways, the canals and in particular the Seine which remained unbelievably forgotten at the time when it was thought that only history was capable of helping us to construct towns."[49]

47. Yves Lion, "Projet urbain: l'architecte peut être aussi un médiateur," interview with Dominique Boudet, *Le Moniteur architecture AMC*, No. 90, June/July 1998, p. 50–52.
48. Yves Lion, "Projets parisiens," p. 32–33.
49. Yves Lion, presentation text, *Grand prix d'urbanisme*, 2001.

Plan for for housing blocs, Thermopyles neighbourhood, Paris, 14th arrondissement, Paris, 1997–2000, on the left, the block built by Léonard & Weissmann architects.

Office building, Avenue d'Italie, Paris, 13th arrondissement, 1993.

Study for Paris' gates: aerial view of the scheme proposed for Porte de Saint-Cloud, 1989.

Porte d'Italie, scheme projected across the Périphérique freeway extending the office building on Avenue d'Italie, Paris, 13th arrondissement, 1989, aerial view.

This idea of entering into a dialogue with Paris through designs for large territories rather than for individual plots legitimated a change of scale in the projects, and in particular a rehabilitation of high-rise buildings, somewhat discredited in Paris since the urban renewal schemes of the 1970s. Between the tower built at the Porte de Saint-Cloud and those proposed for the Masséna-Bruneseau quarter, there were various other high-rise projects, tending to take the form of a blade or a slender slab rather than of a tower. The project for the Paris-Villemin School of Architecture at the Gare de l'Est, a blade-like building clad in marble and located orthogonally to the Boulevard Périphérique at the Porte d'Italie, and the large elevated crescent of the project for the Conference Centre on the Quai Branly, all contributed to the creation of as many platforms leading to the discovery of urban horizons[50]: in echo to *Paris vu par*, these projects and the forthcoming Pole for Oriental Languages and Civilisations, Paris is meant here to be seen from and through architecture.

50. Yves Lion, "Projets parisiens," p. 34–35.

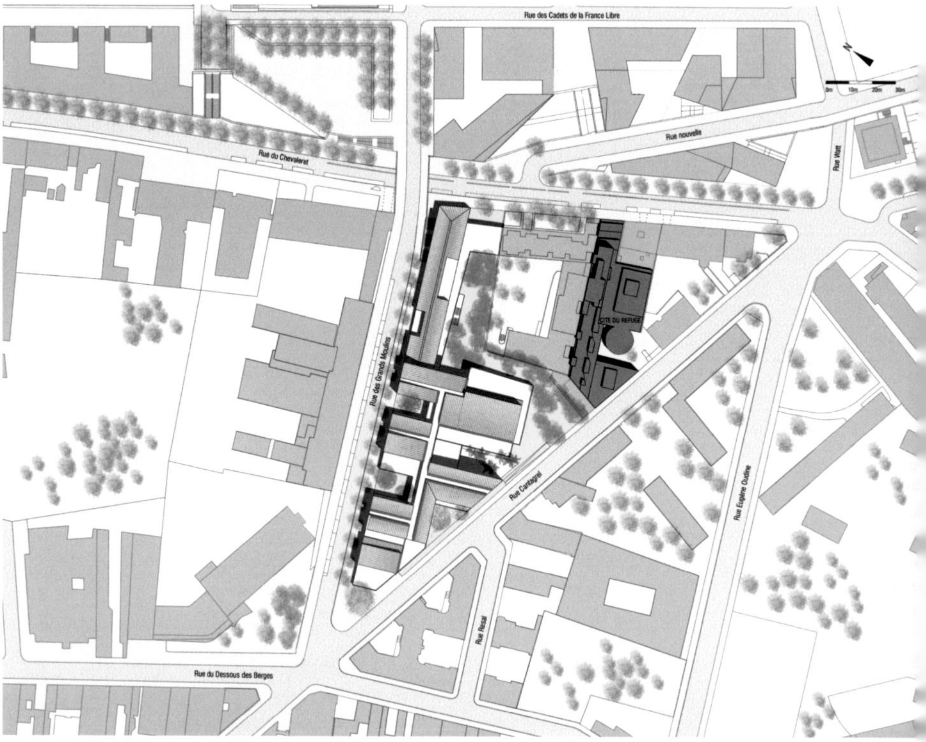

ʾole for Oriental Languages
ınd Civilisations, Zac Paris
Rive Gauche, Paris, 13th
ırrondissement, 2004, Le
Corbusier's Salvation Army
ɔuilding is shaded; view
rom the Pont des Moulins
on the left side, Le Corbu-
ier's Salvation Army and
ts extension by Georges
Candilis); and the proposed
orner bistrot (perspectives
ɔy Lou Kat).

Chapter Five
Suburban air(s)

Between the composed and nevertheless diversified texture of Paris and the less restricting expanses of the new towns, a significant part of Yves Lion's urban engagement is devoted to the suburbs of large cities. To a larger extent than the historical city the suburb represents a practical schooling in urban composition, and for reasons linked to the French policies for commissioning architectural projects and urban plans, for Lion's generation the suburbs were a fertile ground for studies and interventions. Beginning in the 1970s, this generation was guided by a certain populism, directing attention to the styles and ways of life in the suburbs.

Lion's visits to the garden cities of Germany and central Europe doubtlessly led to his ability early on of proposing alternatives to the logic of large housing complexes with which he had grappled since the Vigneux project in 1977. But studies like the one in 1980 for "urban renewal without a plan" in the Hincmar area in Reims familiarised him quickly with a suburban morphology hardly considered until then in France. In this case, the notation of superimposed functional and formal systems led him to advocating a form of discontinued intervention by individual projects along Rue de Venise, resulting in an authentic urbanisation of this rather loose texture. Reading and interpreting the regularities and the peculiarities of suburban landscapes in order to extract from them principles of intervention was the working process inaugurated by these initial contacts with the banlieue, which were not limited to the Paris region. When called on to work with Paul Chemetov, Michel Corajoud and Marc Mimram on the development of the new town of Tama, to the west of Tokyo (1992–1993), Lion surprised and somewhat vexed his Japanese partners by underlining the importance of preserving cabbage and turnip fields between the buildings as elements of suburban identity.

It was not until the 1990s that the office became involved in urban plans of a larger scale. Somewhat conspiratorial reflections of the group 75021, originating from an "Appeal for a Metropolis called Paris" in 1988, entailed criticism of the official town-planning and proposed instead "to begin with all the villages and town quarters that compose the metropolis and thus find its totality."[51] In this spirit, Lion proposed "to mobilise all energies in order to overcome the separation of city and suburbs while forgetting the centre to some extent," in short "to weave a link, with open arms."[52] He formulated a programme towards "re-opening a discussion on the city's fabrication," judging architecture's "constructive or stylistic singularities" to be "derisory" in this context. For him, and in opposition to the determinism of French post-war urbanism, the planner's work consisted of "permitting the liberty of others, i.e. the developers and their architects." For him, "as long as there is no collective agreement regarding this open attitude, as long as some architects are adulated in the name of the originality of their objects, it will not be possible to reproach bad developers for calling on bad architects to make bad buildings. [...] We have to be capable of planning and building with their bad objects and with singular objects, with these solitary machines."[53]

51. Yves Lion, presentation text, *Grand prix d'urbanisme*, 2001.
52. Yves Lion, "La géographie contre l'histoire," *L'Architecture d'aujourd'hui*, No. 253, October 1987.
53. Yves Lion, "Comment faire la ville? Entretien avec Yves Lion," p. 125–126.

Planning study for the Tama area, Tokyo, 1993, general plan.

Urban analysis of a section of Reims, for the "urban renewal without a plan," 1980.

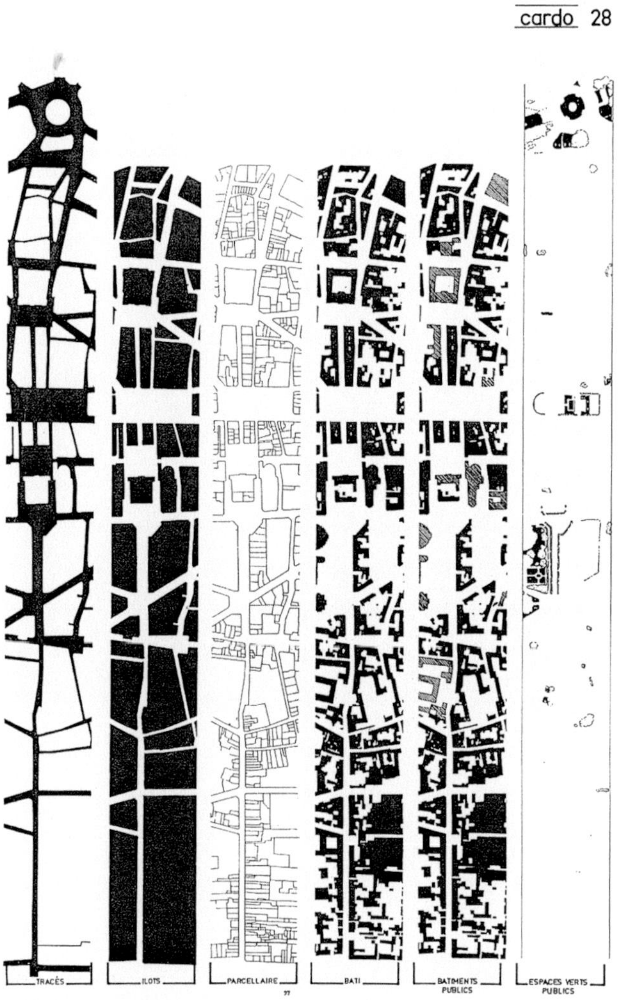
cardo 28
TRACÉS
ILOTS
PARCELLAIRE
BATI
BATIMENTS PUBLICS
ESPACES VERTS PUBLICS
77

It was for the redevelopment project of Saint-Denis Plain that ten years of studies and negotiations with the public authorities, businesses and architects resulted in the formulation of a working method founded on the primacy of the public space. For Lion this is a question of "a public space defining a space of displacement, of dilation, of an extension of the city. A space where time passes, a space which is permanently evolving, which is not subjected to rules dictated by corporate firms that set up facilities there. A space facilitating seduction and hospitality, too."[54] This position of principle was to transform — as a result of consultations and consensus-making — into a working method applied to terrains and various building programmes. Several studies were made on the different means of transport and their inter-modal polarities, nodes for new centres, such as in Choisy-le-Roi, in cooperation with the RER regional train station (1999) in Villejuif, and with the underground stations Villejuif-Aragon (2001) or Rueil-Malmaison, for the creation of a "garden station" (2003).

54. Yves Lion, "Comment faire la ville? Entretien avec Yves Lion," p. 126.

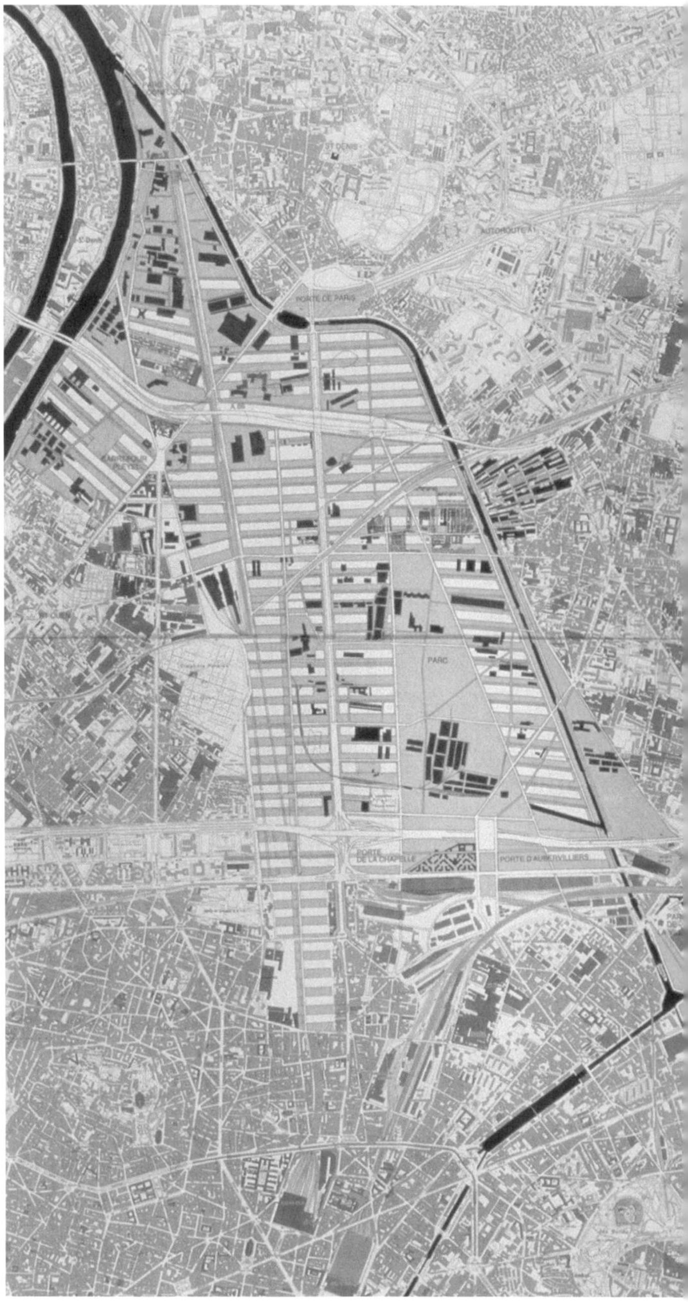

Plan for the Plaine Saint-Denis, layout of public spaces and preserved industrial areas, 1991.

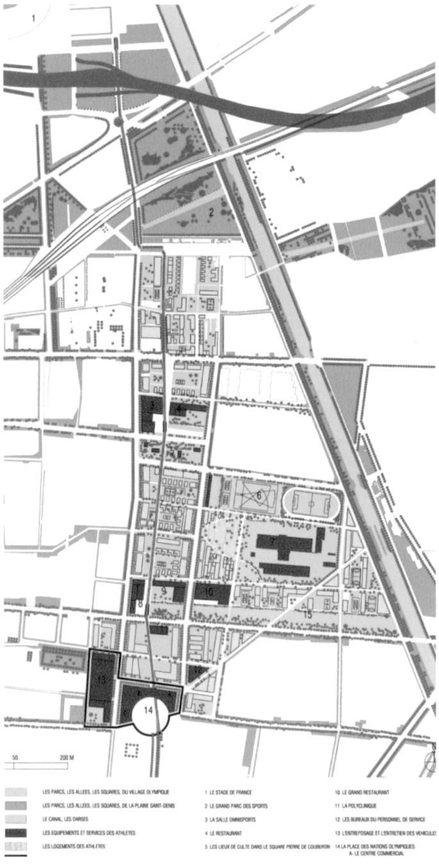

Plaine Saint-Denis, Olympic village for the Paris' 2008 Games candidacy, 2000, plan.

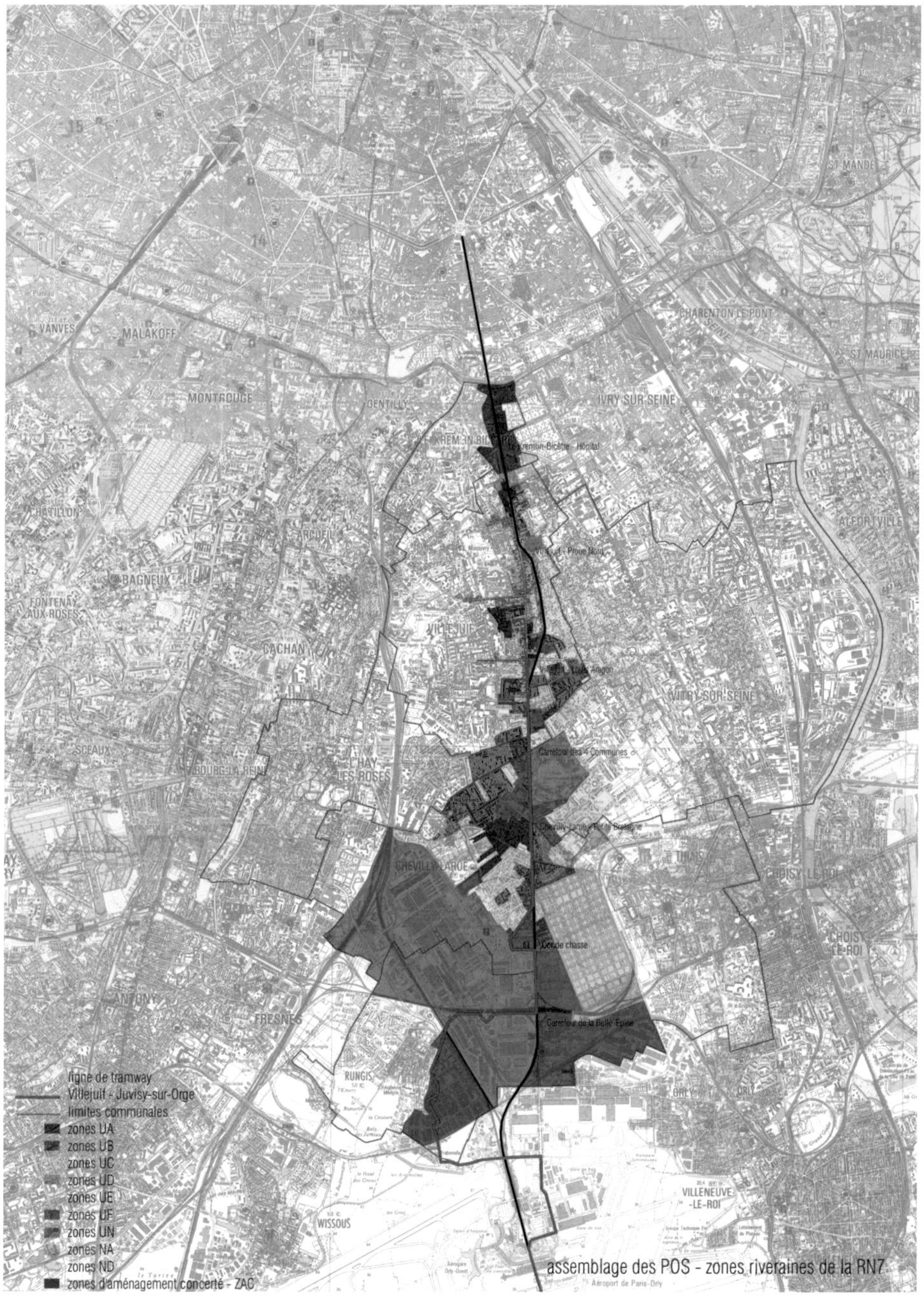

equence of municipal
lanning schemes from
he edge of Paris to the
outhern periphery, 2000.

ransportation node on
lational highway 186,
Choisy-le-Roi, 1999,
he node seen from the
ighway.

Elsewhere it was the historical sedimentation of horticultural or industrial activities and, whenever the case arose, of hydrography that provided material for redevelopment projects. The redevelopment and the subdividing of the Var Plain on the western outskirts of Nice (1999) were dominated by the relation between transport infrastructures and rain water drainage networks. The study for the Grand Pêchers quarter in Montreuil (1999) intervened unfortunately just when the system of walled-in peach-tree gardens had virtually disappeared in this sector. On the other hand, the one for the Chardonnet-Baud sector in Rennes (2001) was still able to consider the presence of agricultural networks and use them to cut up the strips of living quarters separated from each other by impressive hedges.

The post-industrial condition was nevertheless that to which the most intense activity was devoted. The utopian content of the project for the Saint-Denis Plain was unique due to the visibility and relative centrality of its territory within the region, the intensity of the political debate between local authorities and the state and the collegial method used for the planning work. It was a question, as will be seen, of a singular work on urban roadways whose base was an on-going reflection on the specifics of a quarter that had long been a place of immigration and integration. Thus Lion proposed in 1991, at the time of the "Assises de la Plaine" — a series of public meetings where the local constituency was invited to discuss the future — to "safeguard certain living areas which, although timeworn, are the vivid witnesses of successful integration," of "tackling the question of what is sacred" and of "confronting the symbols" of a successful "mestizo culture." For him it was therefore the creation of a large public park, promising a "richer suburb [...], more generous, more tolerant than the town that it is supposed to encircle and, when all is said and done, more attractive."[55]

55. Yves Lion, "Les assises de la Plaine" (Saint-Denis), May 1991.

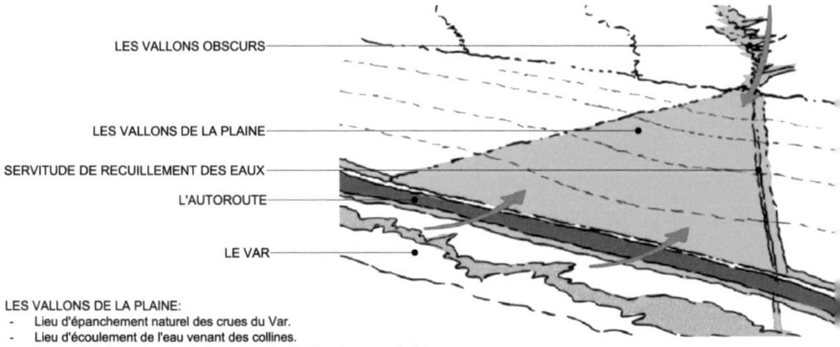
LES VALLONS OBSCURS
LES VALLONS DE LA PLAINE
SERVITUDE DE RECUILLEMENT DES EAUX
L'AUTOROUTE
LE VAR
LES VALLONS DE LA PLAINE:
- Lieu d'épanchement naturel des crues du Var.
- Lieu d'écoulement de l'eau venant des collines.
- Lieu priviliégé pour les eventuels bassins de rétention des eaux pluviales.

Study for the redevelopment of the Var Plain, Nice, 1999, plan and diagram of the use of geography as a defense against the floods.

ransportation node
nd garden-station,
ueil-Malmaison, 2003,
erspective (drawing by
hilippe Drancourt).

tudy for the Chardonnet-
aud sector, Rennes,
001, plan.

Long-term investment on this territory was continued through the enthusiastic preparation of the Paris bid for the 2008 Olympic Games, with the plan for an Olympic village on the grounds of the Plain rather than in the more central location of Les Batignolles, considered by Lion to be "more academic."[56] Compared to the Saint-Denis experience, the elaborated project for the Renault site on the "trapezium" of Boulogne-Billancourt (2001) was a less thematic work, but one in which the slogan of a regulating public space remained valid.

56. *Paris olympiques: douze projets d'architecture et d'urbanisme pour les Jeux de 2008* (Paris: Éditions le Moniteur, 2001).

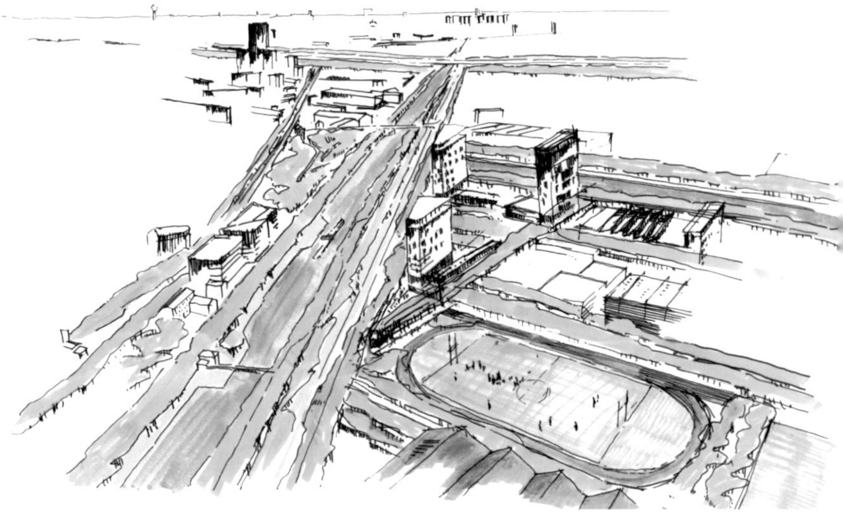

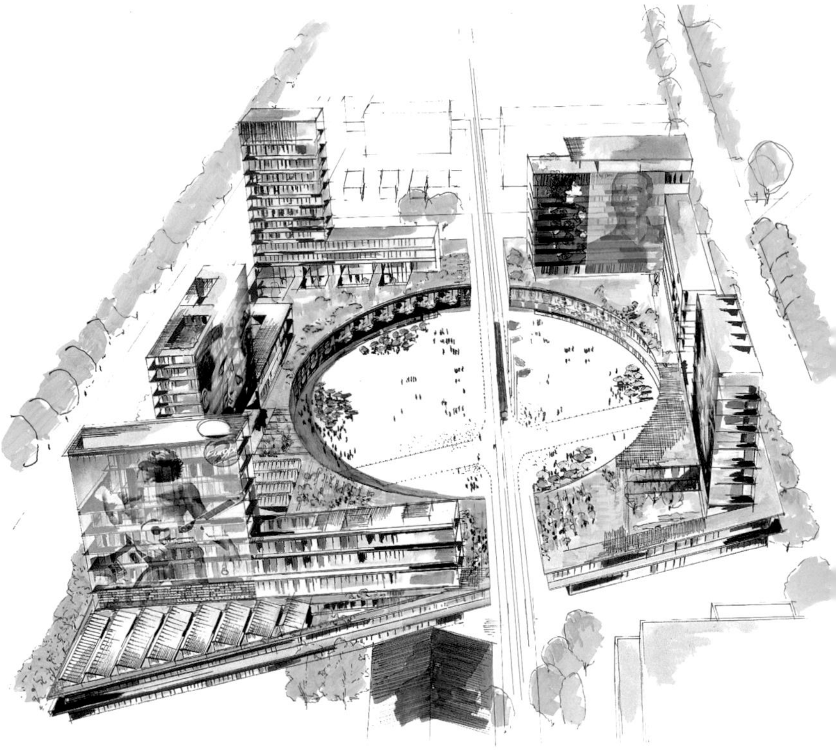

Study for the Olympic village at the Plaine Saint-Denis, 2000, aerial view from the section edging the Saint-Denis canal and view of the Proudhon Gardinoux square.

Planning study for the Renault grounds, Boulogne- Billancourt, 2001, plan and aerial vie

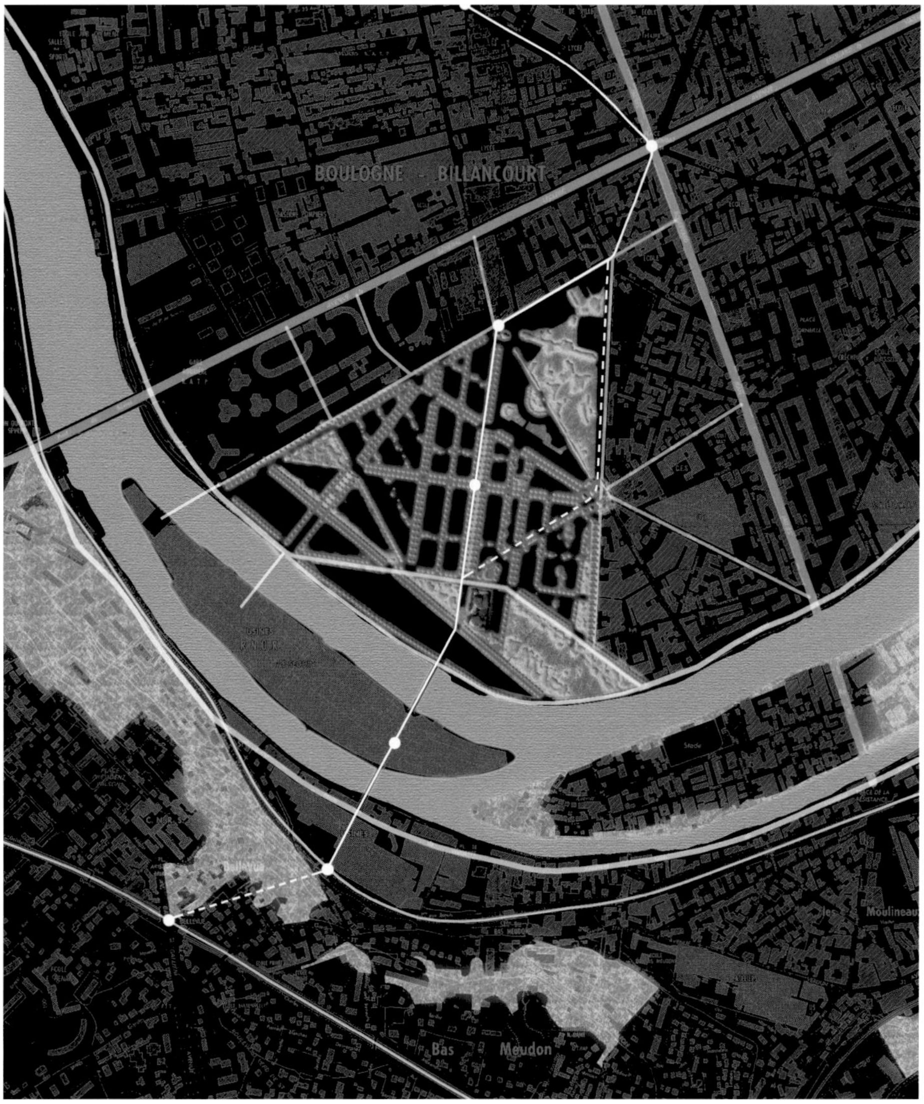
BOULOGNE - BILLANCOURT
Bas Meudon

The policy of the "grand urban projects" launched on a national scale in the 1990s contributed to the multiplication of commissions for the reconstruction of links between the new periphery and historical suburbs. The study of the Neuhof area in the southwest of Strasbourg (2002–2004), where garden cities and low-income estates had a difficult neighbouring relationship, has given rise to a project of reintegrating crafts activities and reinforcing the existing circulation networks to provide the structure for this agglomeration through the radical transformation of the "Cours de la Forêt" into a parkway. Its right-of-way is enlarged and rethought in order to associate diverse types of lanes and public spaces. A work of the same order is launched under the motto of "urban coherence" in Grenoble in 2003–2004, on the outskirts of the Villeneuve new extension built in the late 60s and early 70s.

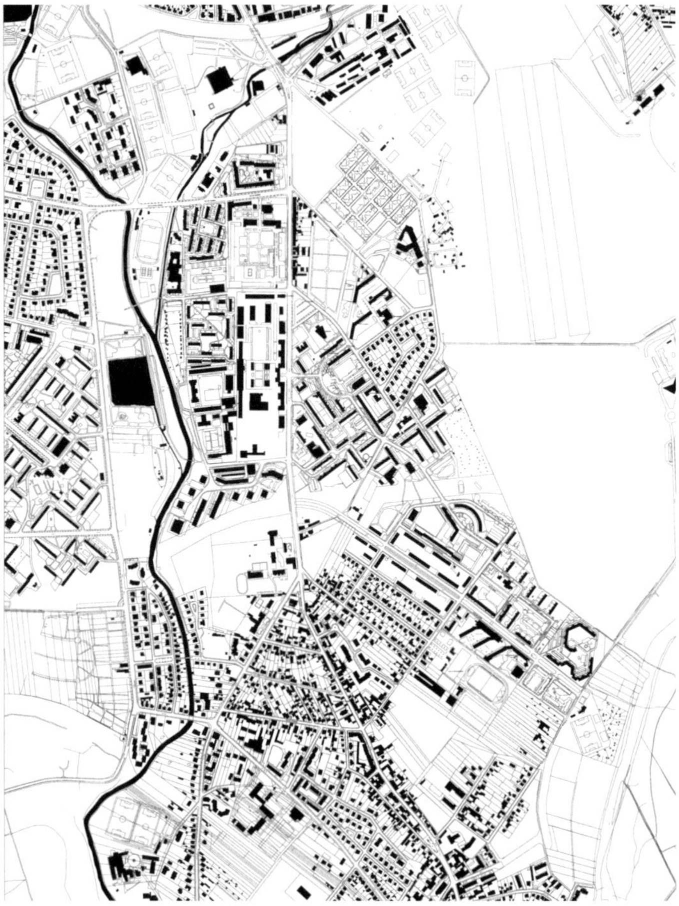

Restructuring of the Neuhof area housing schemes, Strasbourg, 2003, plan of the origina state and plan in 2005.

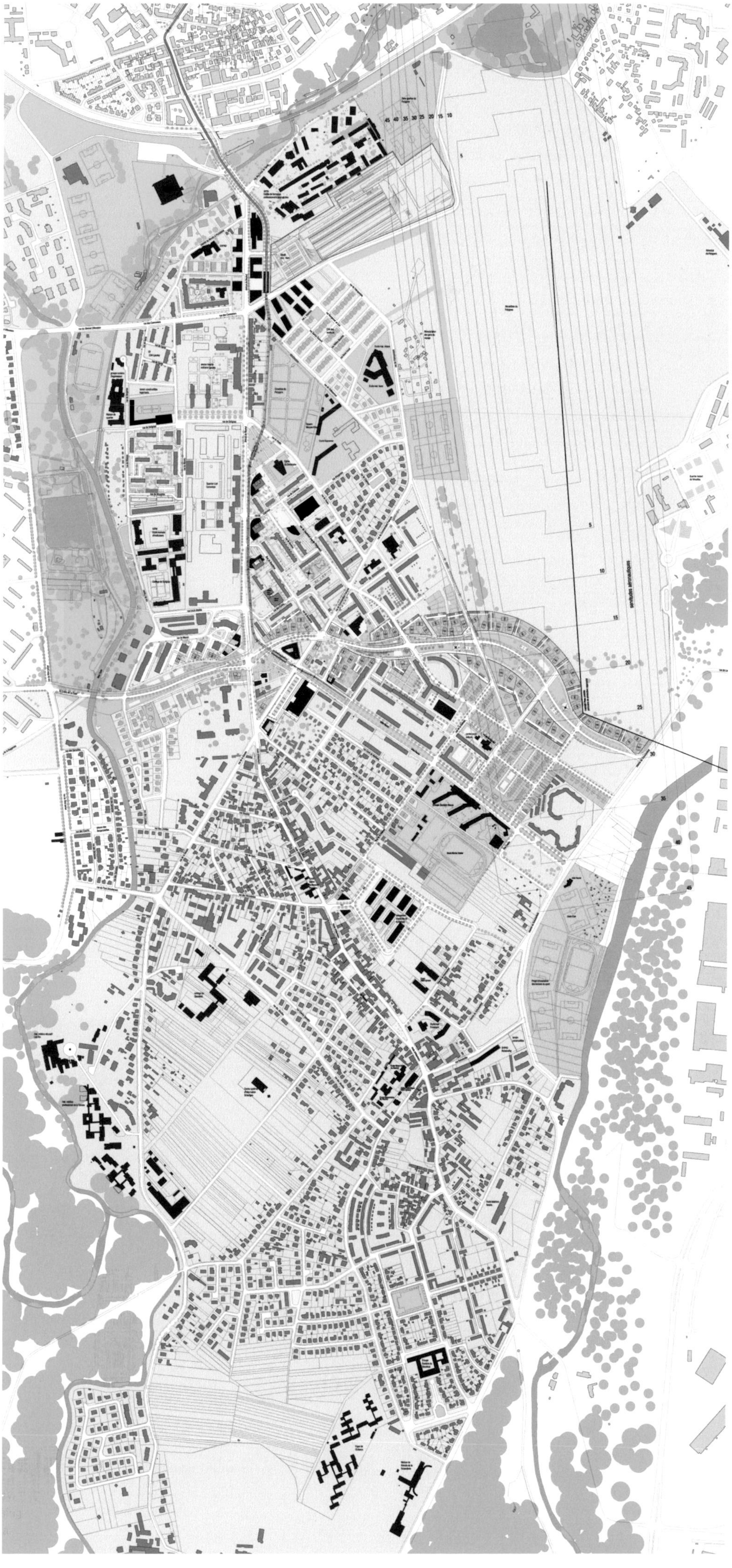

Restructuring of the
Neuhof area housing
chemes, Strasbourg,
004, the Cours de la
orêt transformed into
parkway (perspective
y Lou Kat).

lanning study for
he south of Grenoble,
004, plan.

Chapter Six
Large dimensions

Yves Lion's attention to the potential promise of the density of urban spaces does not lead him to abandon imagining large buildings, which, like most of his contemporaries, he has dealt with in innumerable, exhausting competitions. Earlier than other architects of his generation in France, he has taken up the challenge of public building programmes that demanded a rupture in a way of thinking previously formed almost exclusively around the question of housing. Thus another rapport with society and its rituals informed his architectural thinking true as it is that each of these large building objects spatially transcribes the strategies and the culture of an institution, while at the same time provoking ruptures in scale and texture in the urban landscape.

Much time elapsed before Lion accepted the autonomy of the large monumental object, which only made its return into the discourse of the "Modern Movement" on condition of being associated with a policy of *tabula rasa*. This tendency had already been indicated in *Nine Points on Monumentality*, formulated by Sigfried Giedion, Jose-Luis Sert and Fernand Léger in 1943, a programme doubtlessly more efficient for town planning after the Second World War than the Athens Charter, to which so many failures are ascribed.[57] In many of Lion's early projects his reluctance to leaving buildings isolated was apparent. Thus, the festival hall for Vigneux linked up by way of two long wings to the bulk and the dimensions of neighbouring residences, the Law Courts in Draguignan blended into the horizon of the small town surrounding it, and the large buildings of Nantes were proportioned so as to not surpass the height ceiling of the residential buildings that linked up with them at the centre.

The attention to and the empathy mentioned previously concerning the "déja là" (already there) found its echo in an ability to communicate which led to the interpretation and subsequently to the architectural transposition of building programmes. Thus Lion looked into understanding the human dimension of legal procedures and of the practice of tribunal buildings when he studied the Draguignan Law Courts and those in Lyons. The buildings that resulted were not content with being a loyal interpretation of the programme, be it elaborated in the most professional manner. The public building was conceived as an open place to receive people, between the fulfilment of the programme practices and the non-programmable, and not simply as a place where the monumental presence vis-à-vis other buildings was affirmed.

57. Jean-Louis Cohen, "Les monuments déguisés de l'architecture moderne," in: Régis Debray, ed., *L'Abus monumental* (Paris: Éditions du Patrimoine/Fayard, 1999), p. 215–232.

Palace of Justice, Draguignan, 1983, interior view and entrance patio.

The building in Lyons is a dense assemblage of offices for all members of the judicial institution regrouped in the building slab which spans across the entire plot. The assemblage is characterised for the public by the foyer. It measures the length of the building and provides access to the courtrooms while accommodating the waiting areas. The time spent waiting before or after the trials is frequently laden with emotions and the parties must remain at a distance. Between the impressive but not in the least palatial aspect of the building and the comfort of these spaces, a broad palette of architectural effects unfolds.

Palace of Justice, Lyons, 1995, view from the garden and two views of the main foyer.

In the case of the Convention Centre and the Opera in Nantes, the dissonance of the buildings which forms the base of their monumentality is alleviated by their insertion into the texture of the quarter, something one could call the "domestication" of the two buildings. The two most spectacular effects were the alignment of the convention centre's large vertical glass diaphragm with the planted courtyard which takes pedestrians across from the former LU factory and the contrast between the drum of the opera hall, with its wooden rings of the ambulatories visible behind the glass, and the orthogonal geometry that surrounds it. It is not until one is inside the building that their real size becomes apparent. Unexpected by the visitor, until the envelopment by its wooden walls unfolds its charm, the hall of the conference centre sucks in and distributes crowds, while the opera creates the impression of a turbine triggering a centrifugal movement.

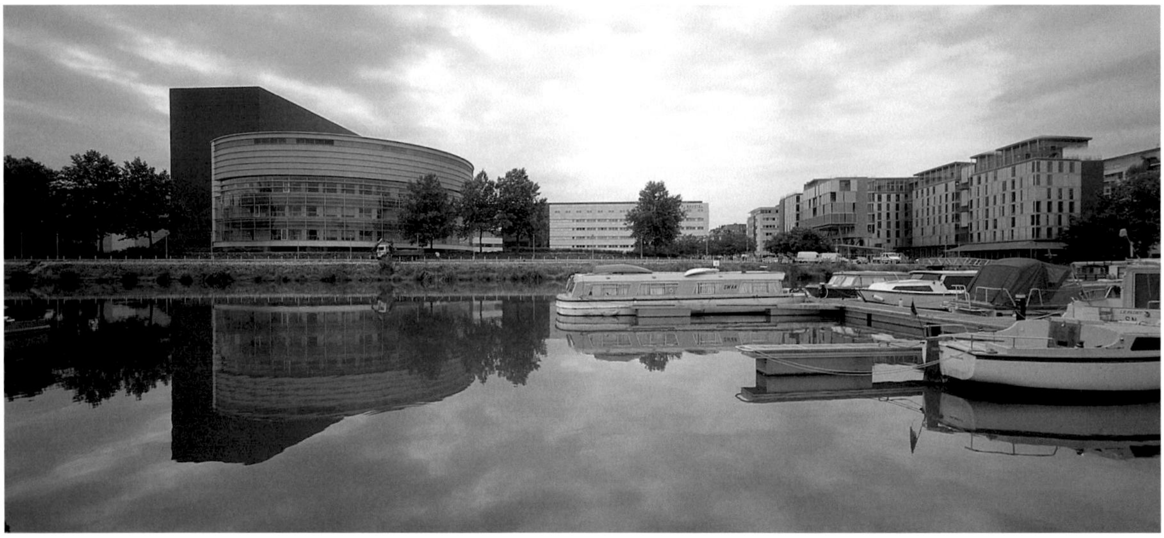

Convention Centre and Opera, Nantes, 1992, view across the Saint-Félix canal and the urban project for the canal's area.

Convention Centre and Opera, Nantes, 1992, views of the Opera's foyer and its 2,000-seat auditorium.

These buildings did not seem to have completely alleviated the frustration following the complete failure of the office's project for the International Conference Centre on the Quai Branly in 1989. Yves Lion would long regret this "simple and reasonable project [...] where all was done so that the conference participant may negotiate war or peace, a project where the activities of international conferences were situated in the lower level of a superstructure resembling three aviaries." In reaction to a zeitgeist which subscribed to "strass and sequins," his aim was to be "normal, radically normal," even in his most important buildings.[58]

It was with a more mundane, more secular programme that he took on something of a larger scale when he wished to relieve high-rise towers, a building programme the French public loves to hate, from their curse. In his reflections on Paris' Boulevard Périphérique he intended "to make a tower at the Porte de Gentilly," without concealing his difficulty in finding the "adequate location." As an example of towers "with a connivance, a complicity with the context," escaping their status as a "hieratic, solitary object," he named the Torres de Parque constructed by Rogelio Salmona in Bogota in 1967.[59]

58. Yves Lion, presentation text, *Grand prix d'urbanisme*, 2001.
59. Yves Lion, "Comment faire la ville? Entretien avec Yves Lion," p. 134.

:ompetition for the
nternational Conference
:entre, Quai Branly, Paris,
'th arrondissement, 1989,
iew from the meeting
ooms and view from the
:iffel Tower.

'roject for a high-rise
uilding at the Porte de
ientilly, Paris, 1991,
erial perspective.

Again and again, the tower poses the problem of monumental singularity. In the project for Amsterdam Zuid (2003–2004), a piece in a master plan engineered by Pi de Bruijn and Kees Christiaanse, the high-rise building designed by the office is not isolated but integrated into a mass plan creating a quarter of "city palaces" equipped with very dense communal services. The mixed programme combines three-level apartments for white collar workers operating from home, social housing and high-end housing, the height of the ceilings allowing for a conversion at a later date. The project escapes simplicity by the continuation of a configuration used by Lion in Paris: the austerity of the street façade contrasting with the landscape of setback floors descending towards the interior of the plot, in a vein that also calls to mind the towers of Latin American coastal towns.

The tower intended for the site at Porte de Gentilly was the first occurrence of this type of building in Lion's planning for the Boulevard Périphérique landscape. The redevelopment project for the Masséna-Bruneseau sector, of which the first version dated from 2001–2002, suggested an order of transition between the adjacent town of Ivry and Paris in which the filter of "small tall buildings" frames the passage of railway lines and the Boulevard Périphérique. In the development of this project in 2003 the towers became one of the three options proposed for the development of the quarter. Only the modification of town-planning regulations, and notably a local suspension of the standard Parisian eaves height of 37 metres, would have permitted the completion of the towers in their most ambitious form. There was a firm intention to endow vertical buildings, much criticised in Paris during the large urban renewal schemes of the 1970s, with a refinement of their urban anchoring. From this point of view Lion favours "the way these objects are placed on the ground, more than the way they radiate into the sky," suggesting that "this really is Manhattan, since there are pedestrians, cars, pavements and shop windows" and that "this is not really the Front de Seine [an infamous Paris multi-level new district built in the 1970s], since there is no harmony between the residual soil and what happens in the sky or on the pedestrian deck."[60] Between these intentions, carried on by a detailed argument on the qualities of towers in terms of durable development and an eventual implementation in built form, the debate with the relevant Parisian communities will be tough, if it is to be judged along the lines of the first bitter exchanges that took place in autumn 2003 and the tentative steps of the mayor of Paris in the matter.[61]

60. Yves Lion, "Projet urbain: des tours pour préserver la ville" (interview with Yves Lion and Xaveer de Geyter by Éric Lapierre), *Le Moniteur architecture AMC*, No. 135, June/July 2003, p. 77.
61. For a review of these debates, see: *Le Monde*, 17 January 2004.

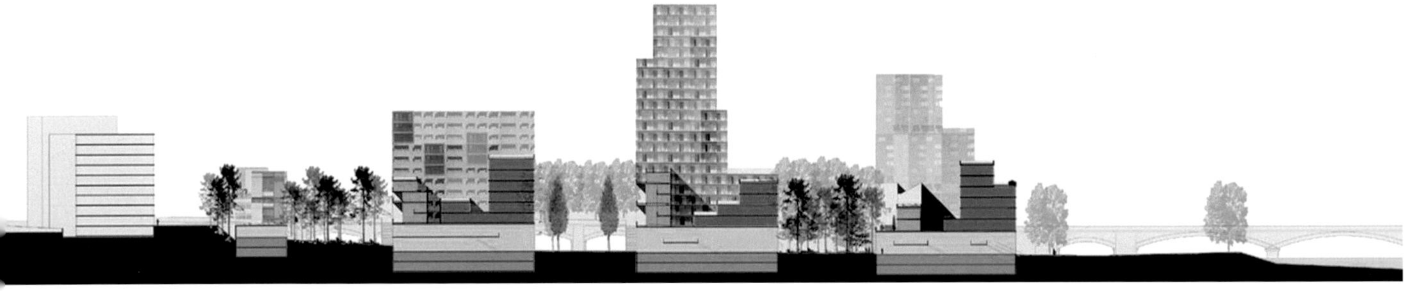

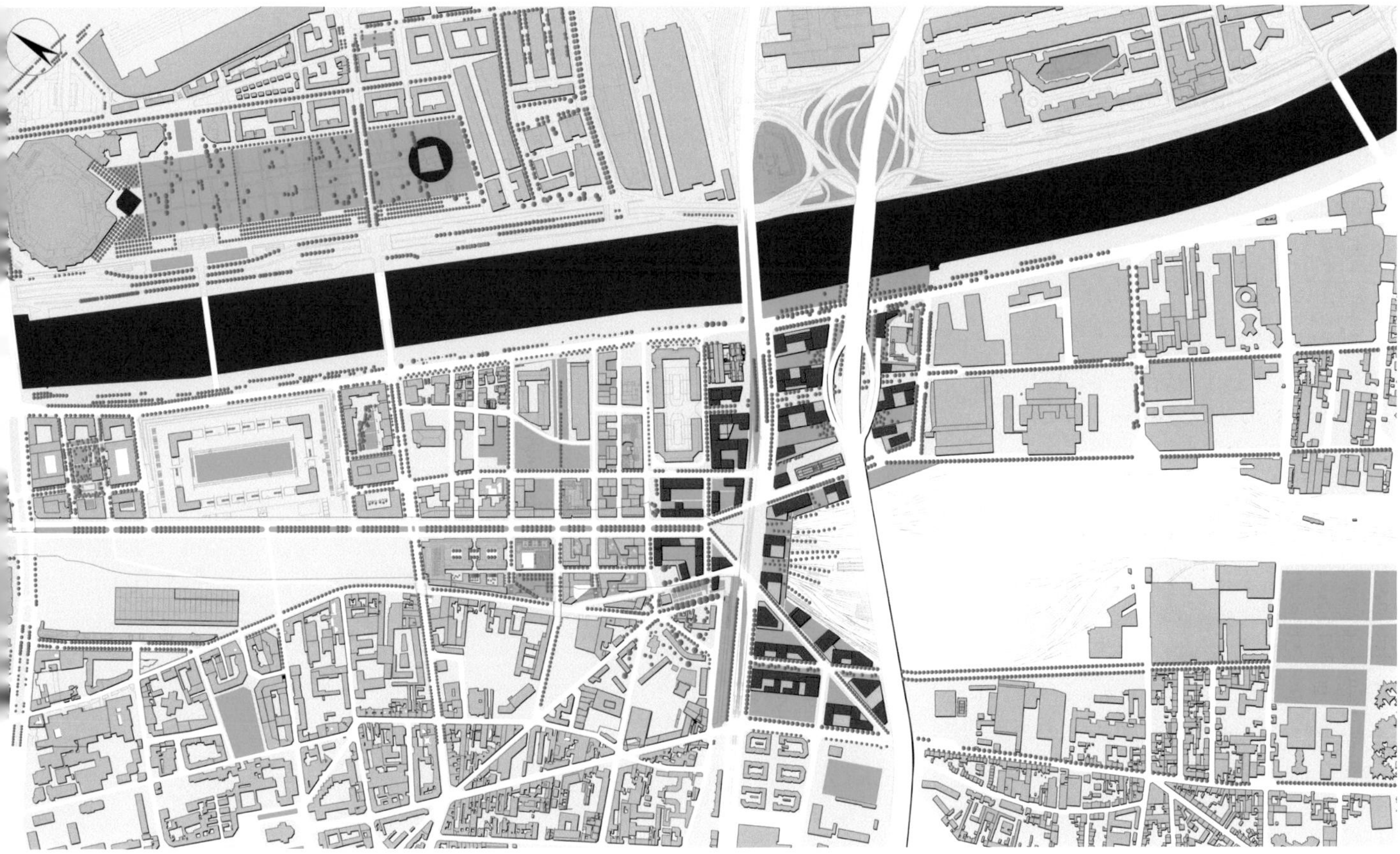

Housing scheme,
Amsterdam Zuid, 2003,
conceptual perspectives.

Paris Rive Gauche,
Masséna-Bruneseau
sector, urban study 2002,
section and plan.

Chapter Seven

From the road to the street

The studio's first projects, in the midst of the period when French urban planning returned to the notion of coherent urban spaces, were wary of rigidly subordinating the building to the existing urban layout. Construction activities in denser textures with their often constraining conditions have imposed the necessity to reflect on this dialectic. Thus it was the case, in the Passage de Flandre, of "tracing a street" merely using architectural components;[62] the renovation project of the Hincmar quarter in Reims was oriented towards the restoration of a coherent, if not continuous, urban façade. In the Vigneux project, dealing with a limited urban area, it was however suggested that, "by playing the game of additions one could organise the continuity, the hierarchy, the reinforcement of the street layout, all sorts of elements borrowed from the city — all this in the hope of allowing for creative social practices, in contrast to the dullness so often commented upon by social scientists working on this type of urban areas."[63] However, in the course of studies for redevelopment, it was the street system itself which became the principal object of the design, the traffic space being seen as an area of mixing and of coexistence between degrees of speed, vehicles and modes of reading urban landscape. The street becomes the public space par excellence, the regulatory system of the urban form.

62. Yves Lion, "Projets parisiens," p. 25.
63. Yves Lion, "Les salles des fêtes de Vigneux," *Architecture, mouvement, continuité*, No 41, March 1977, p. 58.

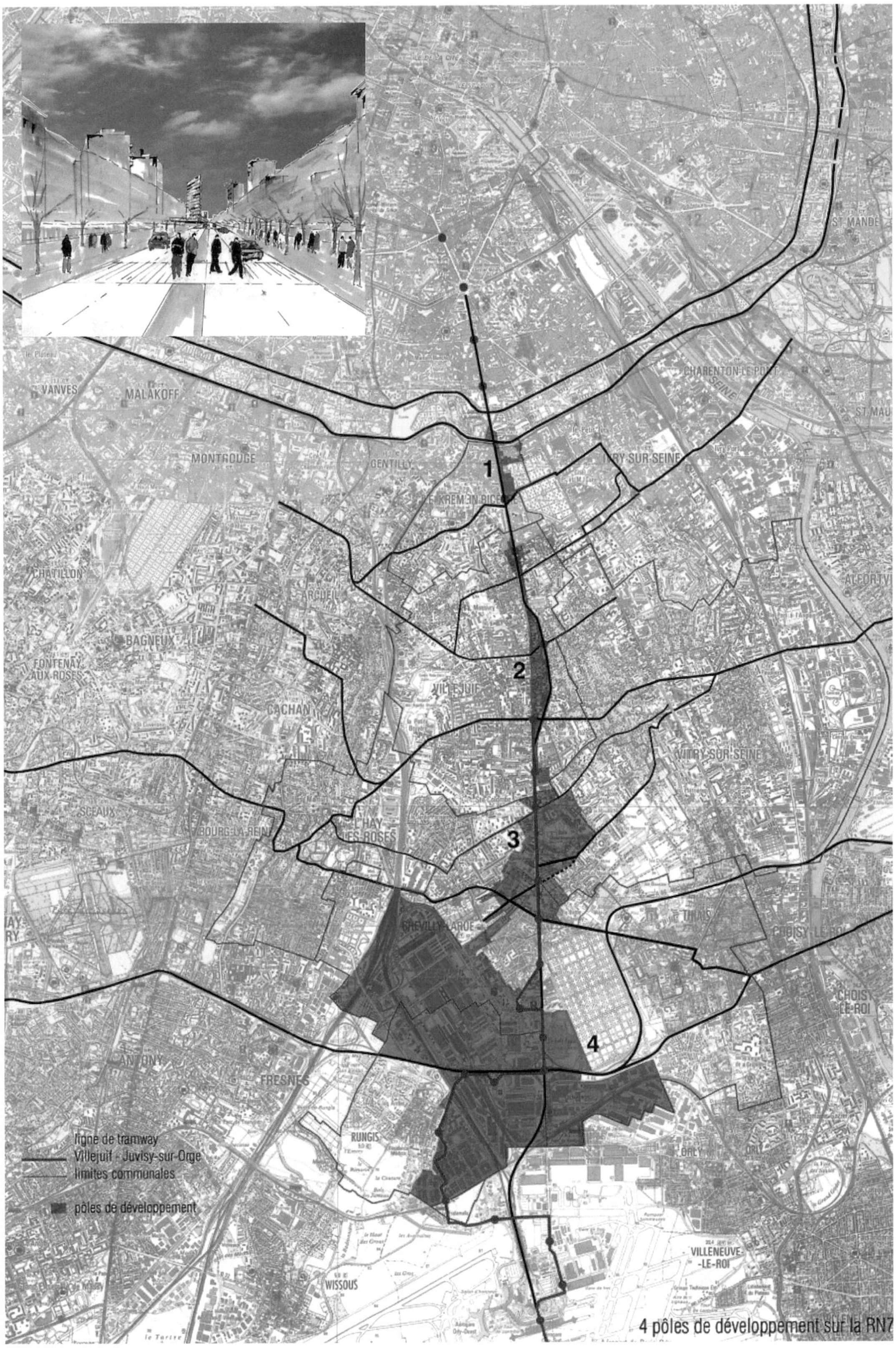

Project for the restructuring of National highway 7, Val-de-Marne, 2001, study sketches and plans.

Some studies were quite singular in their exclusive attendance to roads. This was the case in the work on the Route Nationale 7, to the south of Paris, between the Porte d'Italie and Orly Airport, which tended to define rhythms, sequences of landscape and above all poles of development. The study for the redevelopment of the Boulevard Sud in Saint-Denis de la Réunion (1996), administrative seat of a French-run island in the Indian Ocean, had the clear objective of the overall reorganisation of a nine-kilometre road that described the entire town. This was a town of 150,000 inhabitants whose seafront had been transformed into a motorway; it was a question of making a saturated artery more civilised with two contradicting qualities—that of fluid high-speed traffic and that of good local public transport. These were the expectations of the local authorities. Yves Lion was often able to cite the example of the successful provision of over-dimensioning the highways in Henri Prost's plans designed between 1914 and 1923 for Moroccan towns, permitting them, seven decades later, to accommodate very heavy traffic.[64] But in the redevelopment of an existing road between two inflexible façade lines the organisation of spaces was a zero-sum game. The provisions made for parking spaces were at the cost of mobility, if strictly seen from the domain of the road. The work proposed in this discontinued project essentially involved the definition of principal cross-sections and of new relations between the street and its borders, notably by eliminating cul-de-sac access streets to the adjacent blocks.

64. Yves Lion, presentation text, *Grand prix d'urbanisme*, 2001, p. 63.

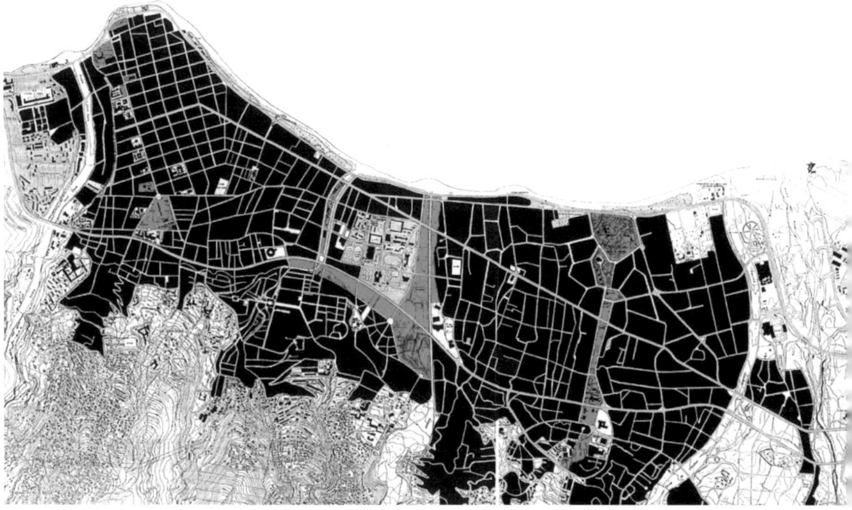

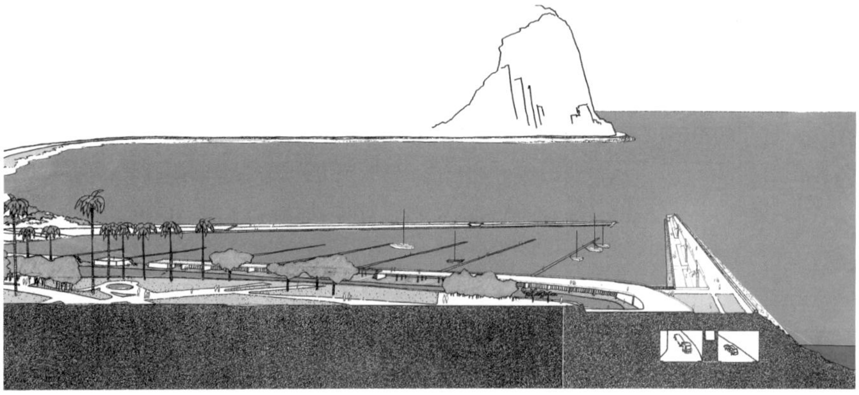
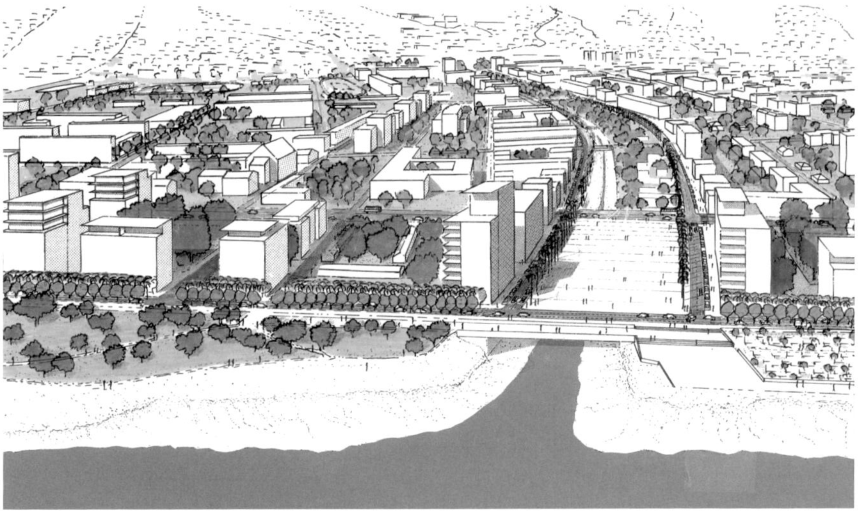
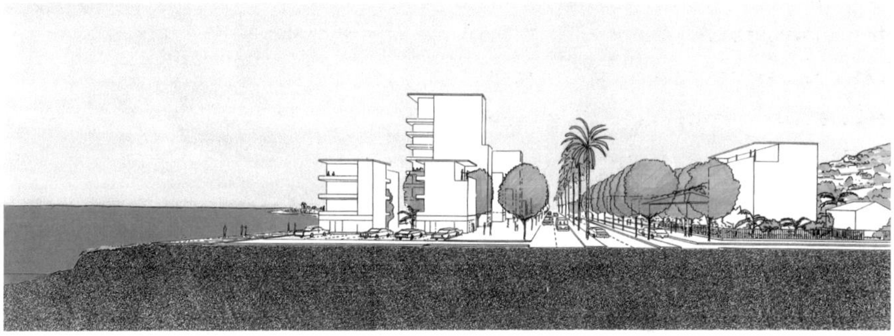

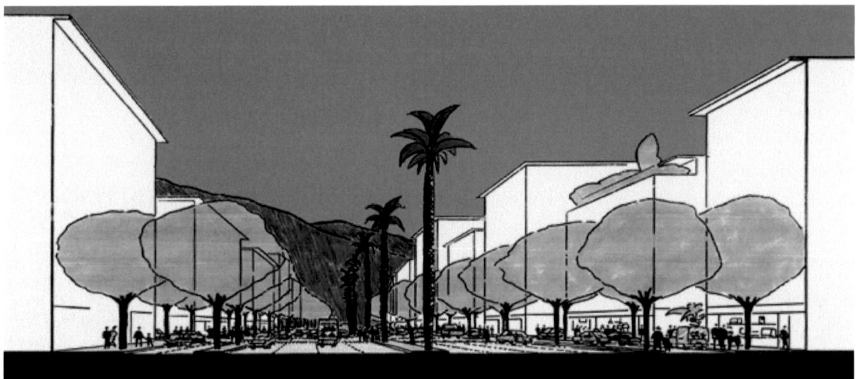

Project for the redevelopment of the Boulevard Sud and the seafront, Saint-Denis de la Réunion, 1996–1997, plan; aerial view; definition of public spaces: view on the harbour; perspective of the Boulevard Sud; and three sections of the Boulevard Sud.

The studies conducted for around a decade on the 800 hectares of the Saint-Denis Plain were also strongly oriented towards the remodelling of roads. Lion responded on his own in 1991 to a competition with a project entitled *50/50* or *The Avenues of the Plain*, in which he suggested a simple rule yet with an inventive implementation to differentiate spaces on which the rules of a public landscape applied and those left to the initiative of each developer. Resumed by the group *Hippodamos 93*, these studies entailed the most spectacular measure, which was the covering of the important axis connecting Paris and the Charles-de-Gaulle airport, namely the trench of the A1 motorway, a considerable wound in the texture of those parts of northern Paris. The new landscape for the areas regained on top of the sunken road was designed by Michel Corajoud. Lion's architectural contribution for the development of the new Avenue du Président Wilson was the construction of service pavilions in brick and metal. The initial abstraction of the grid system soon gave way to a more detailed design for all existing built and landscape elements. The work on public spaces, and in particular the research for a configuration of the road network susceptible to preserving the quarter's open and flexible qualities, could not be solved by the definition of an ideal regulation, as is often the case, but by the discussion of project principles negotiated later with each party involved. The construction of the Stade de France, decided in 1993 with regard to the World Football Cup of 1998, could have overturned the delicate rules of the system, but it precipitated the redevelopment of the canal banks, another structuring axis of the quarter, and demonstrated the flexibility of the principles initially formulated. In 1999–2000, when the study for the Olympic Village 2008 was proposed, the east-westerly axis perpendicular to the Avenue du Président Wilson from the Allée Nozal was the object of a detailed plan in which the attributes for a "comfortable" suburban road were finalised.

The A1 freeway in Saint-Denis, c. 1992, aerial view.

Public spaces built at the Plaine Saint-Denis, 1992, with Hippodamos 93.

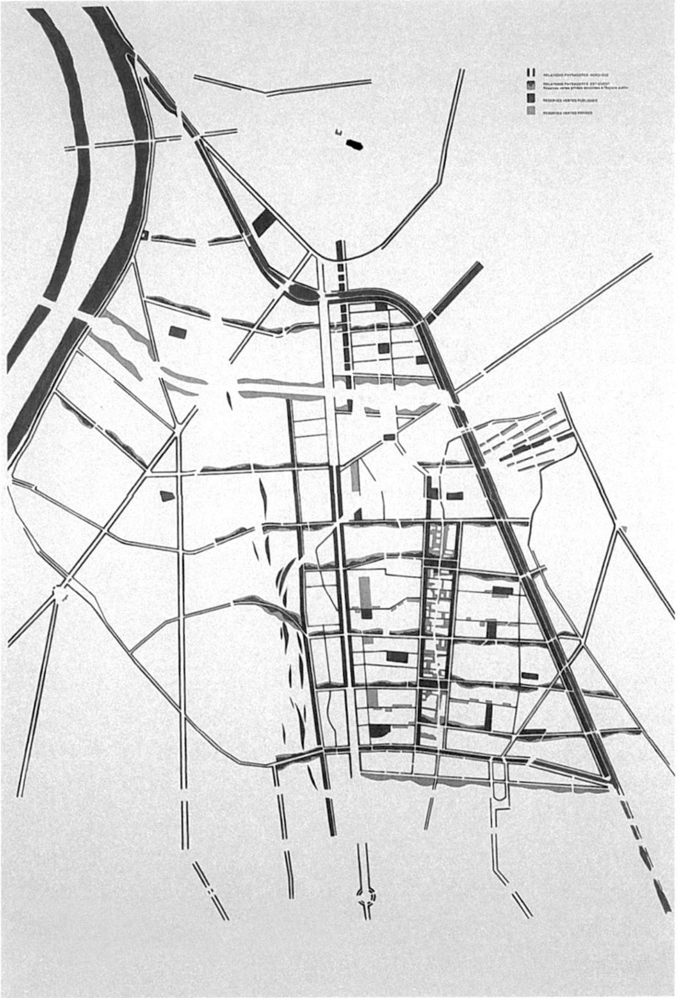

The garden cover of the A1 freeway, Plaine Saint-Denis, 1992, with Hippodamos 93, aerial view.

Public spaces designed for the East/West lanes at the Plaine Saint-Denis, 1992, plan and 1998, perspective.

This investigation of configurations able to combine different modes of mobility, while conserving connections and visual qualities for city dwellers, was continued by other designs, set off by post-industrial conversion or the installation of new infrastructures. In the "trapezium" site in Boulogne the design for the redevelopment of the old subdivisions in Billancourt, absorbed by Renault at the beginning of the twentieth century, tended to render urbanity to roads that had become tunnels between the factory workshops, in particular by the definition of a new nomenclature of intersections and crossroads (2000–2001). In the design for the installation of a new tram system within the road network of Nice (1999) the peaceful coexistence of contradicting modes of transport and movement was likewise at stake. Assuring a minimal speed for the trains, while conserving a capillary for public transport serving the adjacent quarters, was obtained in this case by the adjustment of roadways, pavements and intersections.

Much more radical were the redevelopment projects that had to accompany, domesticate and, at times, pull into question the motorway infrastructures created in the 1970s. In the Masséna-Bruneseau sector in Paris, integrating the Boulevard Périphérique was not achieved through the sneaking in of a road from which an extraordinary spectacle was offered to motorists, but rather by the creation, without nostalgia for traditional Parisian roads and incongruous in this area, of a metropolitan landscape in which the exit of the Quai d'Ivry interchange was reduced and urbanised and the newly created Avenue de France ended. The Boulevard Masséna, on a viaduct at this spot, took on the status of a permeable monument in its lower part — rather like a Roman aqueduct.

existing

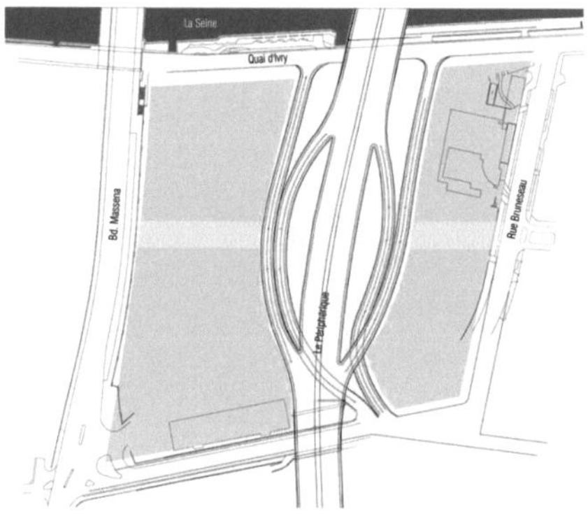

proposed

Paris Rive-Gauche, Masséna-Bruneseau area, restructuring of the freeway interchange, 2002.

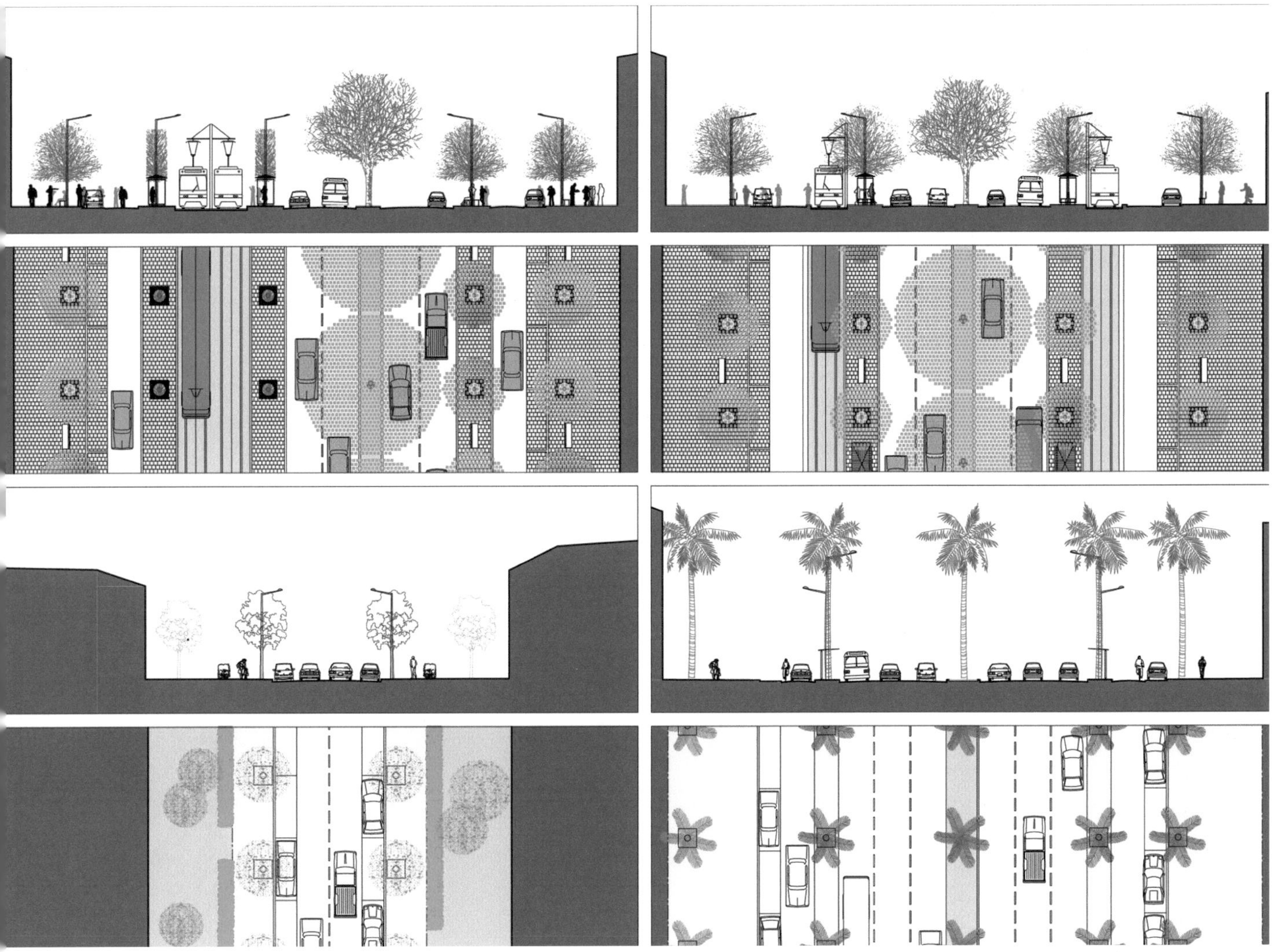

Study for the redevelopment of the Var Plain, Nice, 1999, typical sections of the roads.

Another project with considerable economic and symbolic investment was the development of the Cité de la Méditerranée in Marseilles, the largest public building project in Europe at the beginning of the twenty-first century and planned from 2002. This time the infrastructure consisted both of roads and ports, the question being that of a reconciliation between Marseilles and the modern part of its shoreline, with a very different scale than that of the neighbouring Old Port. Lion's team intended to "avoid sanitised re-conquests" by making tourism only one component of future uses of the territory.[65] The relation between the Quartier du Panier, the Cathédrale de la Major — the rationalist and eclectic chief œuvre by Léon Vaudoyer, until then insulted by the mediocrity of its environment of roads — and the sea is restored by the creation of an esplanade projecting towards the water and at the same time housing the Musée des Civilisations de l'Europe et de la Méditerranée (designed by Rudy Ricciotti) and other commercial premises. Between the Major and the Place de la Joliette, another square that had suffered badly from the civil engineering of the 1970s, the contact between the town and the port was made possible by transferring the logic of the road to the street as soon as the littoral viaduct would be destroyed. Finally, in a third part, in the Arenc area, a concept was proposed for an "inhabited" park that would also accommodate enterprises. Three parallel systems, all corresponding to different practices, will use, if the project is continued, their mutual interference to create the desired pluralities: the urban boulevard, the Boulevard du Littoral and the unrestricted pedestrian flow following the shoreline.

65. Yves Lion, text on study of the definition for *Euroméditerranée*, July 2002.

Cité de la Méditerranée, Marseilles, 2002–2005, restructuring of the seafront boulevard (drawing by Gaël Morin and Olivier Plou), view toward the harbour, and view of the preserved elevated highways (drawings by Gizmo).

Chapter Eight

Urban textures

Defining the character of architectural objects forming the "déja là," for which Yves Lion shows undeniable respect, the plot geometries and the territorial structures constitute a matrix for all interventions and inventions. At the time of the competition for the Maubuée Hills, Eupalinos Corner's team underlined in 1974 that "the logic of implantation gives architecture its role, its domain, its strength."[66] This sentiment of a kind of "geographical necessity," which, as Lion admits, derives from "certain essential readings" from the 1970's, such as that of *Territorio dell'architettura* by Vittorio Gregotti, was maintained by the "intense intellectual complicity" that linked him to his "landscape architect friends" Michel Corajoud and Alexandre Chemetoff.[67] This intimacy with the issues that have profoundly renewed thinking on urban space in France and other parts of Europe is by no means exclusive to Lion, but he is more radical than many of his peers since he affirmed liking "the view of landscape architects on geography, on the sky and on topography" and "their selective memory of history."[68] This affinity lies at the origin of the project for the Marne-la-Vallée School of Architecture, for which the contribution of Chemetoff and of the philosopher and critic Sébastien Marot were to be essential — precisely on this point.[69]

In the study for the Cité de la Méditerranée, concerning "architectural intentions" formulated to complement urban design rules, Lion distanced himself symmetrically from the "general *laissez-faire*, theorised in the name of the 'emerging city,' of the congestion, the necessary mutations" and vis-à-vis the "attempts to control through scrupulous rulings, most often of a Neo-Haussmannian nature, inflicted upon a nostalgic system of stylistic codes." Rather than defining a "third age of the city" or a "third city," a term suggested by Christian de Portzamparc, he outlined a third voice, that of "connivance, of complicity, of civility," founded on a "solid reconnaissance of sites and a critical stance in regard to contemporary architectural culture."[70]

The "solid recognition of sites" remains a constant position throughout the thirty years of projects presented here and seems to have contributed to the accentuation of the specificity of each project. This recognition resides above all in the identification of urban plot regularities, such as in the buildings of the Bassin de la Villette or other projects in Paris built inside dense blocks. It can lead to a critical reproduction of textures, such as in the design for the bazaar quarter in Beirut, where the strategy was an adjustment between the retail texture and the hidden car park texture in a paradoxical return to the current situation where the grid of reference is written in the ground, *beneath* the buildings. In more suburban situations, such as that of the Var Plain in Nice, there are evidently textures that are still determined by agricultural activities that are to be "recognised," and those imposed by water drainage techniques that are to be adjusted.

66 "Deux hirondelles font peut-être le printemps," p. 43.
67. Yves Lion, presentation text, *Grand prix d'urbanisme*, 2001.
68. Yves Lion, "Comment faire la ville. Entretien avec Yves Lion," p. 126.
69. Sébastien Marot, "L'alternative du paysage," *Le Visiteur*, No. 1, Autumn 1995, p. 54–81.
70. Yves Lion, text for the definition study for *Euroméditerranée*, July 2002.

Competition for the Côteaux de Maubuée in Marne-la-Vallée, 1974, with Eupalinos Corner, model.

Cité de la Méditerranée, Marseilles, 2002, aerial view of the J4 jetty as planned (drawing by Gizmo).

Competition for the reconstruction of the bazaar quarter, Beirut, 1994, general plan.

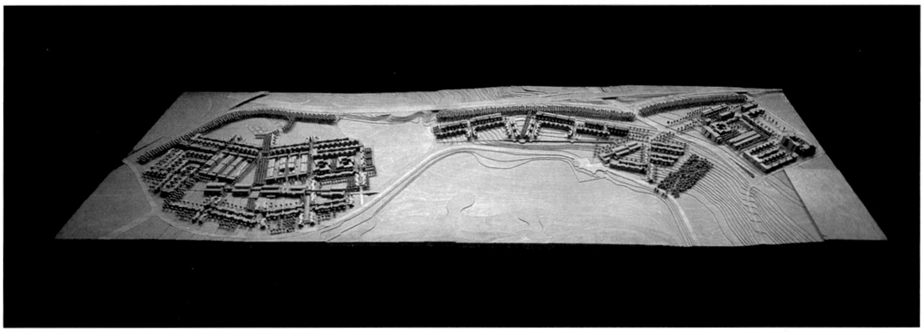

With regard to the "reconnaissance" of preliminary terrains for the interventions, there is nothing innocent about the military origin of the metaphor. As underlined by Yves Lacoste long ago, "geography is first of all at the service of war."[71] Such a position implicates therefore the compilation of map-making materials, but also their cross-reference with patient terrain work, then the confection of interpretation drawings corresponding to these three domains of military art which are, according to Carl von Clausewitz, the strategy, tactic and the conduct of combat operations. The attention towards landscape textures, from the explicit to the more implicit, finds its meaning in each of these domains, as revealed by the designs for the Saint-Denis Plain or the Cité de la Méditerranée. On a strategic scale it is a case of identifying the existing real-estate patterns, the modes of ownership and usage that correspond to them and to their specific plot structure and their functions, in order to fix sequences and prescribe the uses of the principal sectors. On a tactical scale, it is a question of determining interventions in their rapport to the ensemble, but also in their building bulk, through a finer and more critical reading of "pre-existences." Finally, on the scale of operations, it is the identification not so much of grids than of textures permitting the instillation of a precise design perspective without any obligation to mimeticism.

The "critical stance in regard to the state of the culture of contemporary architecture" evoked in the case of Marseilles leads less to the celebration of astounding isolated buildings than to a reflection on the relation between the objects, "as though, deep down, what happens between things is as important as the things themselves."[72] The figures of contemporary art and music, founded on the manipulation of closeness, of distance, of assonance and dissonance, are evidently present in the background of Yves Lion's position, but this "between-things" must also be heard in human terms. As clearly shown by the delicate negotiations carried out with town planners, politicians and Paris associations on the Masséna-Bruneseau sector, and also by the experience of micro-urbanism in the Rue des Thermopyles, this consideration of space "between" objects cannot be limited to a study in terms of composition, eminently sensitive as they may be to the "déja là" or to the territorial texture. It will not escape the risk of running aground in the general incomprehension and in the narcissism of those involved, as experienced by Yves Lion, only in the condition of revealing and of reinforcing the texture of human relations, which are the very fabric of the city.

71. Yves Lacoste, *La Géographie, cela sert, d'abord, à faire la guerre* (Paris: François Maspero, 1976).

72. Yves Lion, presentation text, *Grand prix d'urbanisme*, 2001.

Paris Rive-Gauche, Masséna-Bruneseau sector, urban study, 2002, insertion in the broader context of Paris and the Seine.

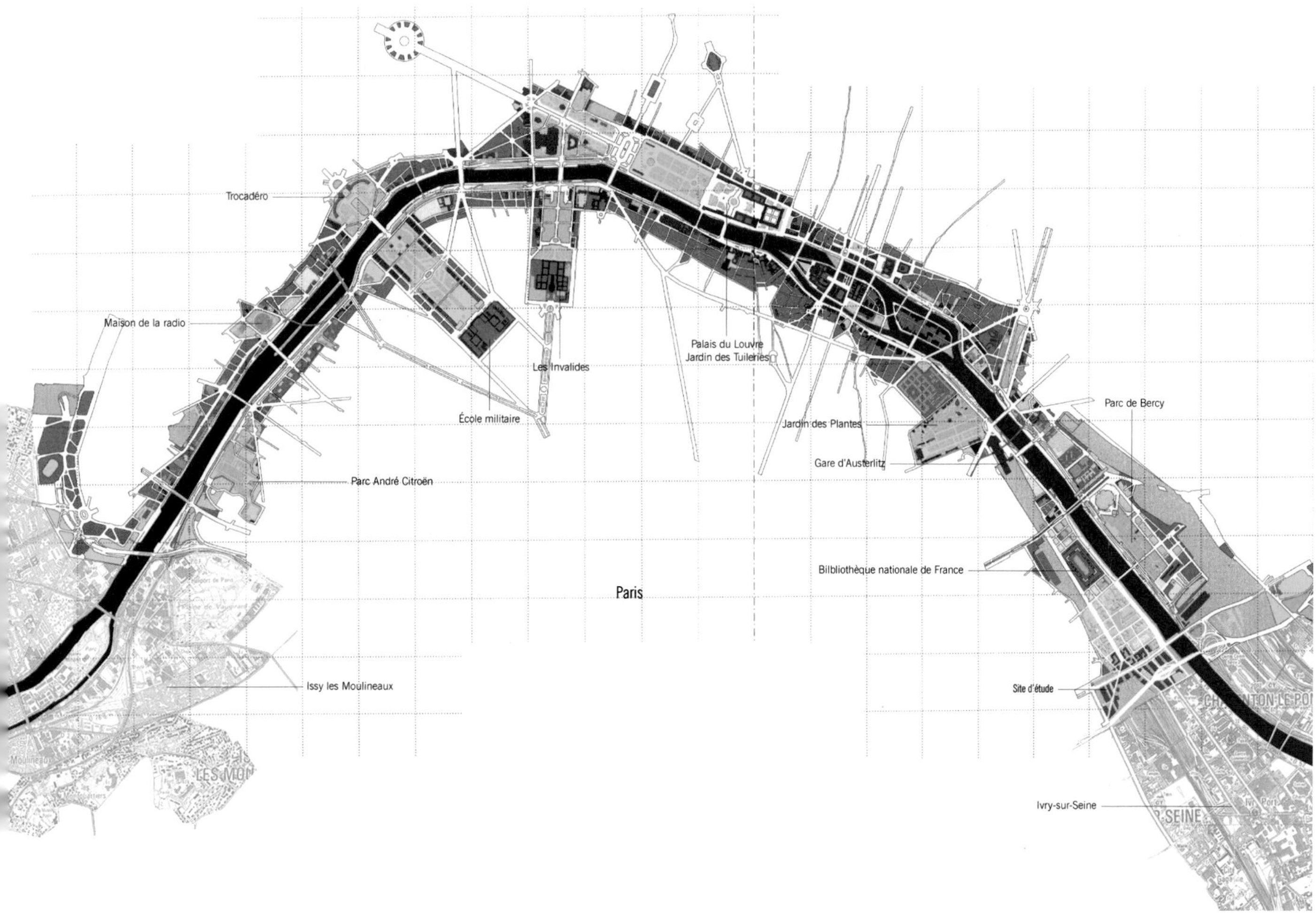
Trocadéro
Maison de la radio
Les Invalides
École militaire
Parc André Citroën
Palais du Louvre
Jardin des Tuileries
Jardin des Plantes
Gare d'Austerlitz
Parc de Bercy
Bilbliothèque nationale de France
Paris
Issy les Moulineaux
Site d'étude
Ivry-sur-Seine

La Cité de la Méditerranée
Marseilles
2001

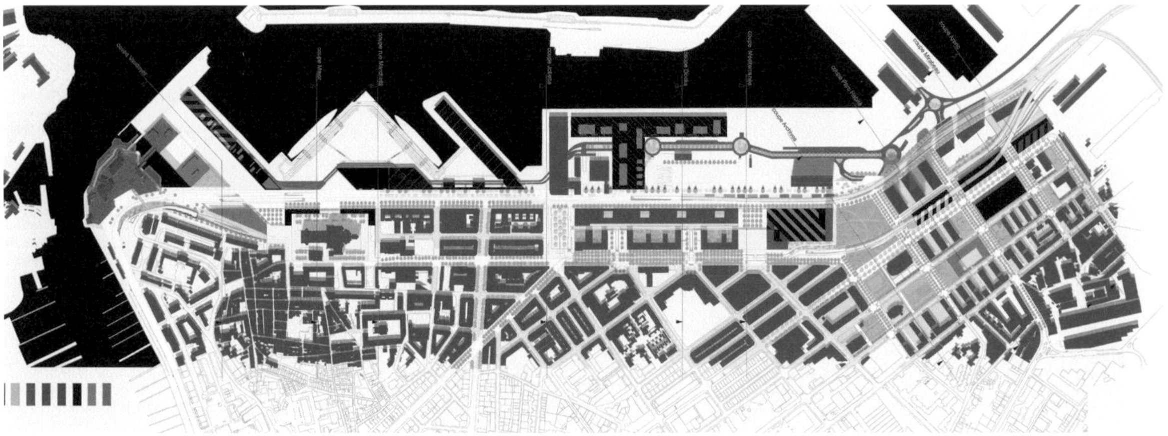

Strategic scale
Establishing through three main sequences the new link of Marseilles with the harbour and the sea.
Arenc: an inhabitable park where life can be harmoniously drifting from work to residence.
From Arenc to the Saint-Jean fort: the harbour as a link between everyday life and exceptional events.
From the La Major cathedral to the Saint-Jean fort: a homage to Mediterranean civilisation.

Tactical scale
At the scale of the harbour, at the scale of the commercial and leisure centre, the experience of a slope transgressing the limit (perspective by Gaël Maurin and Olivier Plou).

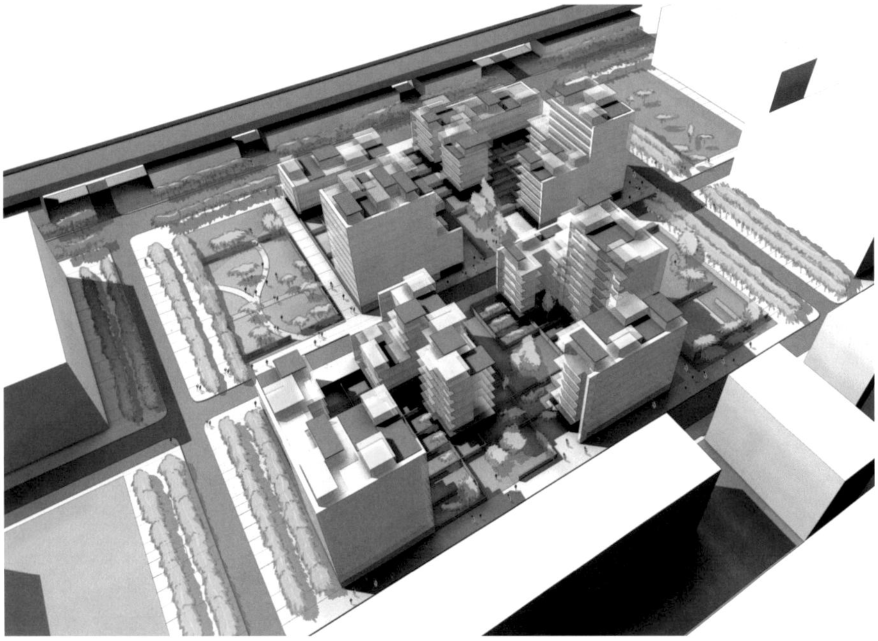

Operational scale
An airy urbanism, at the contact of the harbour's industrial areas and of the neighbourhoods.

Paris Rive-Gauche
Masséna-Bruneseau
2001

Strategic scale
At last, a possible reconciliation between Paris and the periphery.

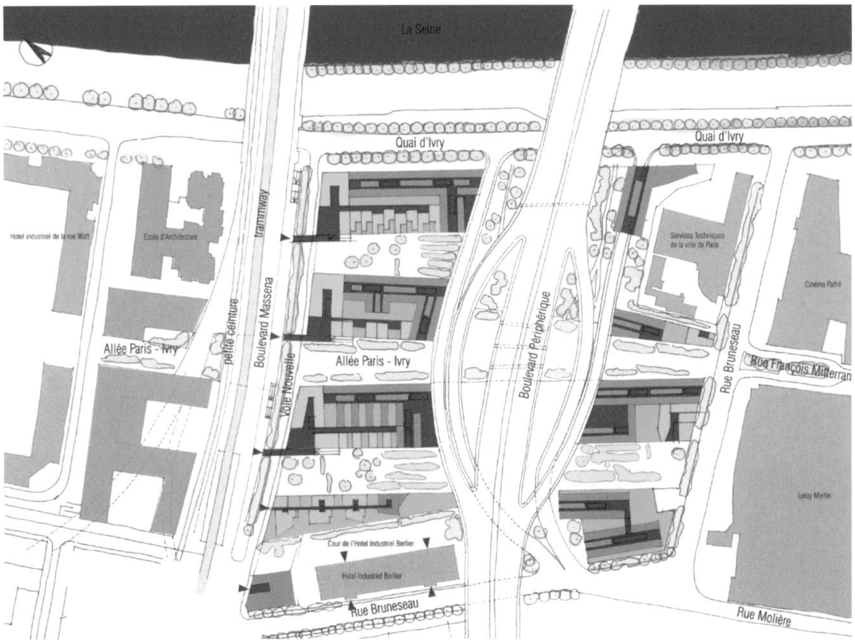

Tactical scale
Acknowledging the Périphérique freeway as a potential space of development, developing its features as a condition of urban comfort.

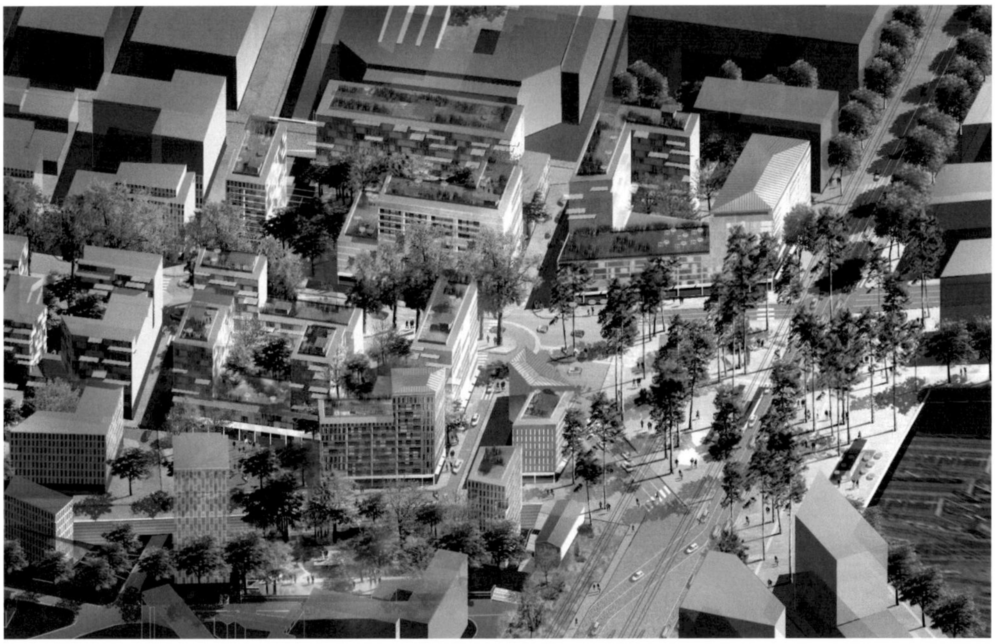

Operational scale
The spaces at the end of the new Avenue de France is devoted to everyday pursuits (perspective by Lou Kat).

La Plaine
Saint-Denis
1992–2002

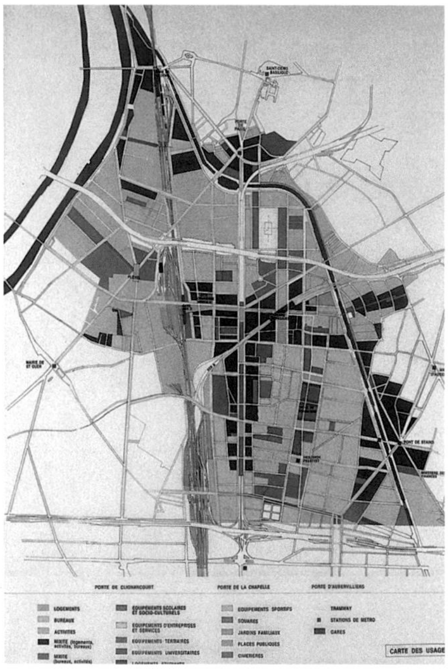

Strategic scale
A mapping of uses and infrastructure.

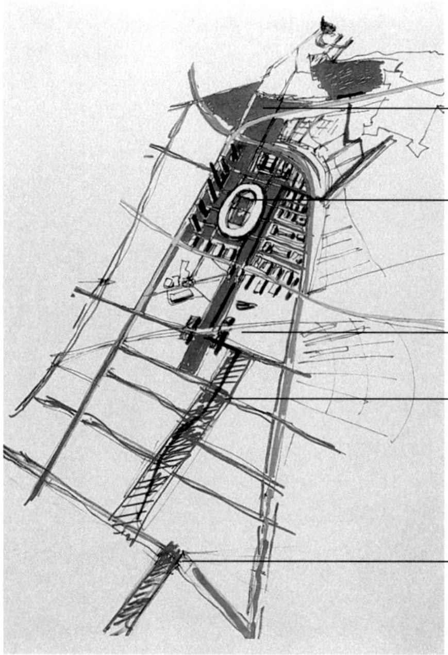

Tactical scale
The Stade de France is inserted in the sequence of the major north-south urban spaces.

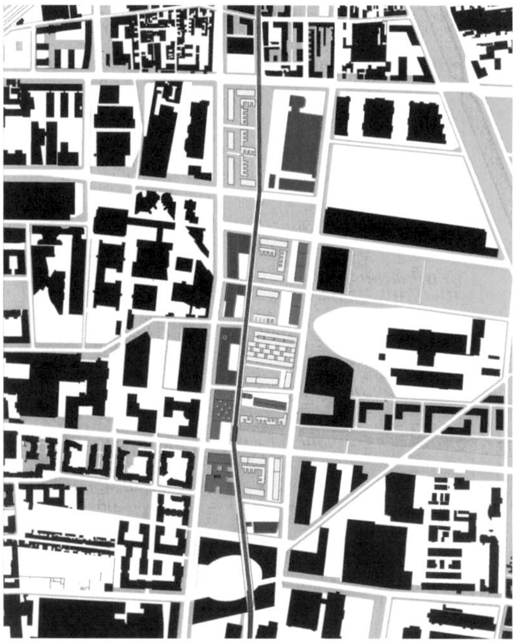

Operational scale
The "Plaine de la Plaine": building inter-municipal links following the bordering territories.

Le Neuhof
Strasbourg
2001

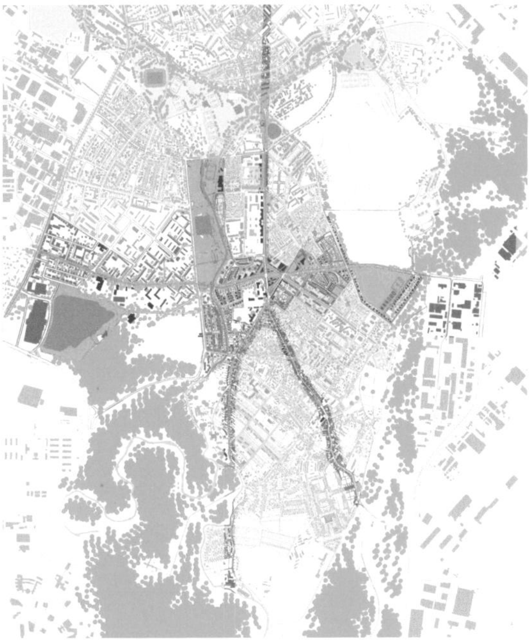

Strategic scale
Establishing a new relationship with the forest, the other neighbourhoods; introducing diversity in the housing supply thanks to the recomposition of public space.

Tactical scale
The Reuss crossroad, main feature in the centrality of the area (perspective by Lou Kat).

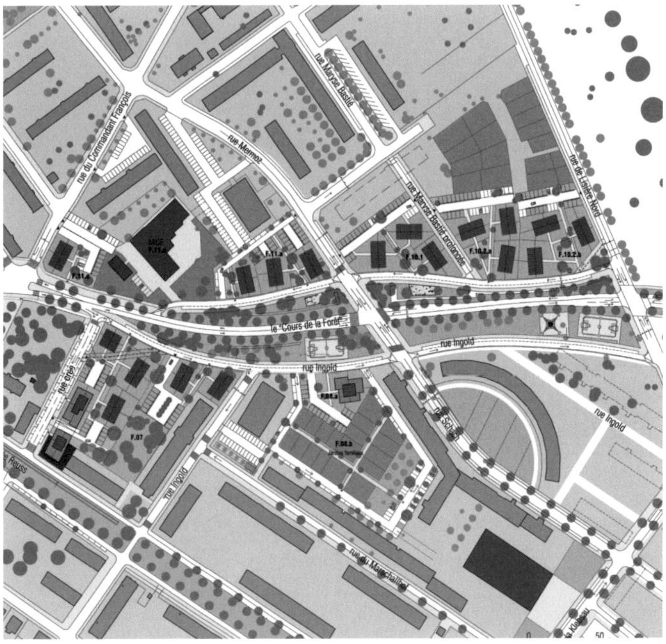

Operational scale
Alongside the "Cours de la Forêt", large Alsatian houses and courtyard housing.

The Ateliers Lion architectes urbanistes were created on January 24, 2003. The founding partners are:
Isabelle Chlabovitch, David Jolly, Sojin Lee, Etienne Lénack, Yves Lion, Claire Piguet

The studio's team in fall 2004.

Selected projects and built works

The projects prior to 2003 are listed by year of completion. Studies and long-term projects are listed by year of their beginning, except when stated otherwise.

1974
Marne-la-Vallée: "Maubuée Hillside." Competition for 3,000 housing units (with Eupalinos Corner; 2nd prize).

1975
L'Isle d'Abeau, new town: "Saint-Bonnet-le-Lac." Competition for the urban development of 10,000 housing units and the construction of 2,500 housing units (with A.U.A. and Eupalinos Corner; 2nd prize).

1977
L'Isle d'Abeau: Urban master plan for the South Plateaux district. Client: EPIDA.

Experimental study on the theme "Open Proportions and Industrialization." Client: Ministry of Cultural Affairs.

1978
Reims: Competition for the construction of 300 housing units and facilities in the Croix Rouge priority development area.

1979
Paris: International consultation for the development of Les Halles district.

1980
Reims: "Renovating without an urban master plan." Preliminary study for the historical centre of Reims and the Hincmar quarter. Clients: City of Reims and Plan Construction.

1981
L'Isle d'Abeau: 66 residential housing units. Client: OPAC du Rhône.

1982
Rochefort-sur-Mer: 30 residential housing units. Client: SCIC Bordeaux.

Reims: Building with 12 housing units and shops. Client: SEDMA.

1983
International consultation for the development of the "Tête Défense," with the International Centre of Communication and two ministries.

Guyancourt: Primary school. Client: SAN Saint-Quentin-en-Yvelines.

Draguignan: Law Courts. Client: Département du Var, Ministry of Justice (with Catherine Degas and Daniel Tajan; special award from the jury of the Équerre d'Argent in 1983).

1984
"Domus demain," study on housing at the beginning of the 21st century, Plan Construction (with François Leclercq). Client: Plan Construction.

1986
Paris: "Language and Communication," Department of the National Museum for Sciences, Technology and Industry of La Villette. 4,000 m^2 exhibition space, overall scenography and detailed planning. Client: Museum of La Villette.

Noisy-le-Grand: 134 housing units. Client: OPAC, Val-de-Marne (finalist for the Équerre d'Argent award in 1986).

1987
Paris, 19th arrondissement: Artists' atelier complex, Passage de Flandre. Client: RIVP – City of Paris Housing Authority (finalist for the Équerre d'Argent award in 1987).

1989
Paris, Quai Branly: Competition for the International Conference Centre. Finalist. Berlin. International consultation for the urban development. Clients: City of Paris, City of Berlin.

Paris, 14th arrondissement: Office building, Rue Didot. Client: SCI, 29 Rue Didot.

Saint-Quai-Portrieux: Vocational school, Côtes d'Armor. Client: Regional Council of Brittany (Public architecture award in 1986 and finalist for the Équerre d'Argent award in 1988).

Blérancourt: Museum of Franco-American Cooperation. Client: Ministry of Culture (with Alan Levitt; Équerre d'Argent award in 1989 and "Marble Architectural Award" in 1993).

1991
Nîmes: Competition for the urban development of the Montcalm Square near the arenas, followed by several urban studies. Strasbourg: Competition for Rhine area and Strasbourg-Kehl east-west axis.

Tangiers, Morocco: Study for the development of the historical city centre around the Grand Socco square. Client: City of Tangiers.

Tangiers: House. Client: Yves Lion.

Paris, 19th arrondissement: 108 housing units, apartments for a retirement home and activity facilities. Bassin de la Villette. Client: RIVP – City of Paris Housing Authority (finalist for the Équerre d'Argent award in 1991).

1992
Nantes: Convention Centre and Opera with 2,000 seats. Client: City of Nantes (with Alan Levitt; finalist for the Mies van der Rohe and the Équerre d'Argent award in 1992).

Villejuif: Complex for 80 housing units. Client: OPHLM, Villejuif.

1993
Berlin: Competition for the Reconstruction of the Royal Palace.

Paris, 13th arrondissement: Office building, Porte d'Italie. Client: RIVP – City of Paris Housing Authority.

1994
Beirut: International competition for the reconstruction of the Souks in the Beirut city centre (special jury award).

Paris: 90 subsidized low-cost housing units in the mixed housing development zone of Bercy. Client: City of Paris, SAGI.

1995
Paris, 14th arrondissement: House. Client: SCI Macydo.

Marne-la-Vallée, Cité Descartes: 200 housing units. Client: OPAC, Val-de-Marne and Expansiel.

Lyons: Palace of Justice. Client: Ministry of Justice (with Alan Levitt; finalist for the Équerre d'Argent award in 1995).

1996

Madrid: Competition for the rehabilitation of the Prado Museum.

Paris, 4th arrondissement: European House of Photography, Hôtel Hénault de Cantobre. Client: City of Paris and SAGI (finalist for the Équerre d'Argent award in 1996).

Paris, 16th arrondissement: Conversion of an office building into 67 housing units, Rue Boileau. Client: RIVP – City of Paris Housing Authority (finalist for the Mies van der Rohe award in 1996).

1997

Geneva: Competition for the Museum of Ethnology.

Ljubljana: Competition for the Sports Centre complex of Ljubljana.

Saint-Denis de la Réunion: Competition for the restructuring of the sea side and for the master plan of the Boulevard Sud. Clients: City of Saint Denis, Regional Council.

Paris, 15th arrondissement: Conversion of an office building into 78 housing units, Boulevard de Grenelle. Client: RIVP – City of Paris Housing Authority.

Boulogne-Billancourt: Master plan for the city centre (6 hectares). Guest consultation for the construction management of the mixed housing development zone in the city centre. Client: City of Boulogne-Meunier, Coprim.

Sainte-Geneviève des Bois, Essonne: 72 housing units for private ownership. Client: Arc Promotion II.

Sainte-Geneviève des Bois: 66 subsidized, low cost housing units. Client: SCIC AMO, Travail et Propriété.

1998

Aubervilliers: 70 housing units for private ownership. Client: Arc Promotion II.

Paris, 1st arrondissement: Percier Fontaine and Duchâtel Halls at the Louvre Museum. Client: Louvre Museum (with Alan Levitt).

Saint-Denis: Roofing of the A1 highway, service pavilions. Client: Département Seine-Saint-Denis (with Alan Levitt).

1999

Nice: Development for the Var Plain (850 hectares). Urban study. Client: City of Nice.

Paris, 4th arrondissement: Urban development for the Schomberg block, Quai Henri IV: Conversion of three former barracks buildings by J. Bouvard into 77 social housing units. Client: OPAC, Paris.

Construction of 128 housing units for the Republican Guards. Client: Ministry of Defence (with Alan Levitt).

Paris, 18th arrondissement: Institute for the Education and Training of Image and Sound Professionals. Client: FEMIS and RIVP – City of Paris Housing Authority.

Paris, Porte des Lions: Second entrance to the Louvre Museum and museography of the Spanish and Italian painting halls. Client: Public administration for cultural building projects (with Alan Levitt).

2000

Nice: Project for the harbour and its district. Client: City of Nice (with Laurent Hodebert).

Choisy-le-Roi: Val-de-Marne (60 hectares). Study for a multi-modal node. Client: Council of Val-de-Marne; DDE 93; Mayor of Choisy-le-Roi.

Paris, 18th arrondissement: 50 housing units on the Francœur block. Client: RIVP – City of Paris Housing Authority.

Pantin, Seine-Saint-Denis: Elaboration of the urban master plan (2.8 hectares) for the mixed housing development zone of Villette Quatre Chemins. Clients: City of Pantin, SEMIP.

Paris, 14th arrondissement: Urban study for the Didot-Thermopyles quarter. Client: City of Paris; OPAC, Paris.

2001

Rennes: Competition for Chardonnet-Baud district (60 hectares). Study for the development of an urban project. Client: City of Rennes.

Dieppe: Urban study for the master plan and the development of the Neuville-Nord district. Client: City of Dieppe.

Paris to Orly: National road 7. Urban requalification study for all local authorities concerned. Client: SADEV 94; Département Val-de-Marne.

Boulogne-Billancourt: Urban project for a former Renault site. Client: City of Boulogne-Billancourt; G3A. Boulogne: Privately owned students' and social housing units in the city centre. Client: Meunier Promotion.

Paris, 14th arrondissement: 32 subsidized low cost housing units, mixed housing development zone of Montsouris. Client: SAGI.

Vitry-sur-Seine, Val-de-Marne: Elaboration of the urban master plan (4.5 hectares) and the programme for the mixed housing development zone of Port à l'Anglais. Client: SADEV 94.

2002

Plaine Saint-Denis: Urban redevelopment project on 800 hectares. General urban master plan, sector studies for the construction of the Stade de France in 1998, for the World Football Cup and for the Olympic Village, as part of the Paris candidacy for the 2008 Olympic Games. Client: City of Saint-Denis; City of Aubervilliers; Mission Plaine de France; GIP Paris 2008. Project started in 1991.

Villejuif-Juvisy: National road 7 and tramway project. Client: DDE 94.

Beirut: Competition for cultural and sports facilities for the American University.

Louvre Museum: Salle d'Actualité, Graphic Arts department. Client: Public administration for cultural building projects (with Alan Levitt).

Vitry-sur-Seine: 77 housing units for private ownership. Client: Arc Promotion.

2003
Arles: Competition for the construction of an urban parc in former railway facilities. Client: Department Provence Alpes Côte d'Azur.

Marseilles, Port Terraces: Designer-developer competition for the construction of shopping facilities in the Port of Marseilles.

Montreuil: Conversion of an office building into housing units, district of Les Grands Pêchers. Client: Low-cost Housing Authority of the City of Montreuil.

Beirut: French Embassy. Client: Ministry of Foreign Affairs (with Claire Piguet; Équerre d'Argent award in 2003).

Current design and building projects

2001–
Marseilles: Cité de la Méditerranée (200 hectares). Urban study for the harbour site and the city of Fort Saint-Jean in Arenc. Client: Euroméditerranée (with Ilex, Kern, Confino).

Strasbourg, Neuhof district: Great City Projects, Urban study for the redevelopment of the district and construction of public spaces. Client: Strasbourg Community Office.

Strasbourg: Operations for the main lease holders of the city quarter: construction of the public spaces at the Cité Solignac. Client: Habitation moderne. Rehabilitation of 60 housing units with local activity facilities near the building. Client: CUS Habitat.

Paris: Mixed housing development zone Paris-Rive Gauche, urban study for the Masséna-Bruneseau sector. Client: SEMAPA.

2003–
Grenoble: Urban study for the southern districts and initiative for the establishment of public spaces. Client: City of Grenoble.

2004–
Paris, 13th arrondissement: National Institute for Oriental Languages and Cultures (INALCO) and university library for Languages and Cultures (BULAC), mixed housing development zone Paris-Rive Gauche. Client: Regional authority of Ile-de-France.

Paris, 5th arrondissement: Globe Institute of Physics and Library for Universal Sciences. Client: Public authority for urban development of Jussieu.

Damascus: French School. Client: Ministry of Foreign Affairs.

Grenoble: Prospective urban study for the southern districts of the Grenoble agglomeration. Client: Grenoble Alpes Métropole.

Var Plain: Urban study for the development of the Var Plain. Client: Community Office of Nice-Côte d'Azur.

Saint-Denis: Social housing and public facilities, St Denis 93. Client: Sonacotra.

Pantin: Mixed housing development zone of Villette 4 Chemins, 91 housing units. Client: Arc Promotion II.

Vitry: Mixed housing development zone of Port à l'Anglais, 54 housing units. Client: Arc Promotion II.

Vitry: Mixed housing development zone of Port à l'Anglais, urban development of public spaces (road system and park). Client: SADEV.

Marseilles: Mixed housing development zone of La Joliette, block M5 Les Docks, 140 housing units and underground car park. Client: Apollonia (with Castro-Denisof; Pyramide d'Or and Pyramide de Vermeil award for durable housing from the National Federation of Housing Developers).

Bordeaux: Mixed housing development zone of Bastide, 550 housing units and car park and gardens. Client: Apollonia.

Lyons: Mixed housing development zone of Berthelot-Epargne, 450 housing units and facilities. Client: Apollonia.

Rueil-Malmaison: Urban development for a multi-modal node. Client: City of Rueil-Malmaison.

Amsterdam: Study for the construction of a tower with housing units and utilities of 25,000 m^2. Client: Royaal Zuid Consortium.

Blérancourt: Extension for the Museum of Franco-American Cooperation. Client: French Museums Board (with Alan Levitt).

Romainville/Pantin: Rehabilitation of the Romainville castle and the Seigneurie in Pantin, for the urban development project of the outdoor leisure centre of La Corniche des Forts. Client: AFTRP (with Ilex Paysagistes).

Bruxelles: Feasibility study for the restructuring of a city block on Quai Willebroeck. Client: Alco Building.

Beirut: Place des Martyrs competition.

Luxemburg: Competition for the Porte d'Hollerich (with Benoît Moritz).

Bibliography

Monographs on Yves Lion

Yves Lion: études, réalisations, projets, 1974–1985 (Paris: Electa Moniteur, 1985), presentation by Daniel Treiber

Yves Lion (introduction by Alexandre Chemetoff, interview with Pierre-Alain Croset) (Barcelona: Gili, 1992), in English and Spanish.

Articles by Yves Lion

"Eléments d'une réponse," *L'Architecture d'aujourd'hui*, No. 174, July/August 1974, p. 42–44.

"À propos du concours de la petit Roquette," *L'Autre journal d'architecture*, supplement to *Architecture, mouvement, continuité*, No. 1, February 1975, p. 14.

"Une nouvelle monumentalité," *L'Architecture d'aujourd'hui*, No. 175, September 1975, p. 23.

"Une géométrie claire pour un espace appropriable," *Techniques et architecture*, No. 312, December 1976, p. 103.

"Les salles des fêtes de Vigneux," *Architecture, mouvement, continuité*, No. 41, March 1977, p. 58.

"Concours de Rochefort," *Architecture, mouvement, continuité*, No. 42, June 1977, p. 64 (with Daniel Tajan).

"Circonstances," *Architecture, mouvement, continuité*, No. 32–33, December 1979, p. 24.

"Doctrines et incertitudes," *Les Cahiers de la recherche architecturale*, No. 6–7, 1980, p. 61–62.

Une rénovation sans plan d'urbanisme, le quartier Hincmar à Reims, Paris, Plan Construction, 1980; study report, with Alan Levitt and Bernard Althabégoïty.

"Maintenant construire," *Architecture en France, modernité/postmodernité*, Paris, Institut Français d'Architecture/Centre de Création Industrielle, 1981.

"Habiter aujourd'hui," *Architecture, mouvement, continuité*, No. 24, September 1981.

"L'avant-centre," in: *Henri Ciriani* (Paris: Institut français d'architecture/Éditions du Moniteur, 1984), p. 17.

"Un pur et dur si tendre," *Architecture, mouvement, continuité*, 1985, p. 62 (about Riccardo Rodinò).

Domus demain, Paris, Plan Construction, 1986; study report, with François Leclerq.

"L'hommage est ici un travail ...," in: Jean-Paul Robert, ed., *Corbu vu par ...* (Paris: Institut français d'architecture/Liège: Mardaga, 1987), p. 138.

"*Domus demain*, la bande active," *L'Architecture d'aujourd'hui*, No. 252, September 1987, p. 16–20 (with François Leclerq).

"Pourquoi des ruines en guise d'école d'architecture," *Le Moniteur architecture AMC*, No. 17, October 1987, p. 40–41 (with C. Carpente, C. Potet, M. Sebald, L. Tournié).

"Quatre plots passage de Flandre," *L'Architecture d'aujourd'hui*, No. 253, October 1987, p. 36–38.

"La géographie contre l'histoire," *L'architecture d'aujourd'hui*, No. 253, October 1987.

"*Domus demain*," in: Kristin Feireiss, ed., Berlin – Denkmal oder Denkmodell? Architektonische Entwürfe für den Aufbruch in das 21. Jahrhundert/*Berlin – Monument ou modèle de pensée? Projets architecturaux pour l'entrée dans le 21ème siècle* (Berlin: Ernst & Sohn, 1988), p. 172–173.

"À propos d'urbanisme," 1990.

"Les assises de la Plaine" (Saint-Denis), May 1991.

"Liebe Berliner Freunde," in: Kristin Feireiss, ed., *Das Schloss? Eine Ausstellung über die Mitte Berlins* (Berlin, Ernst & Sohn, 1993), p. 122–123.

"Projets parisiens," *Paris d'architectes* (Paris: Éditions du Pavillon de l'Arsenal, 1996), p. 14–39; (lecture given on 2 February l994).

"Qualité architecturale et dimension urbaine de l'habitat," *L'habitat: quels modes de vies, quelles formes urbaines, A & C*, No. 26, July 1995, p. 32–37.

"Opinioni e progetti," *Internazionalismo critico, Casabella*, No. 630–631, January/February 1996, p. 80.

"Au nom de l'îlot et pour lui, un peu de discontinuité," in: *La ville-architecture*, No. 3, January 1997, p. 10–11.

"Viviendas con vistas al Sena," *Francia Fria, Architectura viva*, No. 65, May/June 1997, p. 20–25.

"Hassan Fathy: impression d'Yves Lion," *Urbanisme*, No. 300, May 1998, p. 30.

"Pour une nouvelle école d'architecture des territoires," in: Pierre-Alain Croset, ed., *Pour une école de tendance, mélanges offerts à Luigi Snozzi* (Lausanne: Presses polytechniques et universitaires romandes, 1999), p. 184–187.

"Vie bourgeoise," in: Pierre Gangnet, ed., *Paris côté cour: la ville derrière la ville* (Paris: Pavillon de l'Arsenal/Picard, 1999), p. 49–53.

"Geoffrey Bawa," *Matières*, No. 3, 1999, p. 66–75.

"Architektur und Raum: zum Lehrkonzept der neuen Ecole d'Architecture de la Ville & des Territoires in Marne-la-Vallée," *Bauwelt*, No. 40–41, October 1999, p. 2252–2253.

Presentation text, *Grand Prix d'Urbanisme*, 2001.

"Un projet opérationnel, la nationale 7 entre Paris et Orly," in: Jean-Pierre Pranlas Descourt, ed., Territoires *partagés: l'Archipel métropolitain* (Paris: Pavillon de l'Arsenal/Picard), 2002, p. 322–325.

Introduction générale, *Rendez-vous de l'architecture, transforma(c)tions,"* (Paris: Éditions du Patrimoine, 2002), p. 20–26.

Text on study of the definition for Euroméditerranée, July 2002.

"Architectures savantes, architectures populaires," *Les Cahiers de la recherche architecturale et urbaine*, No. 15–16, July 2004, p. 123–126.

Interviews and conversations with Yves Lion

"Loger ou bien réinventer le monde," *L'Architecture d'aujourd'hui*, No. 252, September 1987, p. 21–23 (conversation between Yves Lion, Jean Nouvel, Paul Chemetov and Renée Gailhoustet).

"Je me sens plus producteur qu'auteur," *Le Moniteur des Travaux publics*, No. 4493, 5 January 1990, p. 56–57 (interview with Odile Fillion).

"Débat autour de la Grande Bibliothèque de France," *Le Monde*, 14 November 1991 (conversation between Yves Lion, Paul Chemetov and Dominique Perrault, conducted by Frédéric Edelmann and Emmanuel de Roux).

"De Franse architectuur boet voor haar gouden eeuw," *Archis*, March 1992, p. 12–16 (conversation between Paul Chemetov, Yves Lion and Gérard Thurnauer, conducted by Frédéric Edelmann and Emmanuel de Roux).

"Comment faire la ville," *Les Cahiers de la recherche architecturale*, No. 32–33, 1993, p. 123–134 (interview with Jean-Jacques Treuttel).

"L'architecture moderne, c'est d'abord et surtout une pratique sociale," *Les grands entretiens du Monde*, Vol. 3, 25 January 1994, p. 64–67 (interview with Frédéric Edelmann and Emmanuel de Roux)

"Une opportunité pour la région parisienne," *La Ville sur Seine*, No. 2, August 1995, p. 139–141 (interview with Catherine Tricot).

"Le Palais de justice de Lyon: un palais côté cour et côté jardin" in: *Le bâtiment public dans la cité* (Paris: Ministère de l'Equipement, des Transports et du Logement, 1998), p. 32–43 (debate between Yves Lion, Vahé Muradian, René Eladari, Robin Sébille and Philippe Monot).

"Projet urbain: l'architecte peut être aussi un médiateur," *Le Moniteur architecture AMC*, No. 90, June/July 1998, p. 50–52 (interview with Dominique Boudet).

"L'espace public doit être l'espace du public," *Le Monde*, 14 November 2000 (interview with Frédéric Edelmann and Emmanuel de Roux).

"Entretien avec Yves Lion," *Aventures architecturales à Paris, l'art dans les règles* (Paris: Pavillon de l'Arsenal, 2000), p. 118–121 (interview with Françoise Arnold).

"Il faut assumer l'héritage urbain," *Le Monde*, 11 January 2001 (interview with Emmanuel de Roux).

Yves Lion, interview with Soline Nivet, June 2002, published in: *La lettre de George V*, 2002.

"Projet urbain: des tours pour préserver la ville," *Le Moniteur architecture AMC*, No. 135, July 2003, p. 74–79 (interview with Xavier de Geyter and Eric Lapierre).

Articles and publications about Yves Lion's work

Marc Emery and Patrice Goulet, *Guide de l'architecture en France, 1945–1983* (Paris: Groupe l'Expansion/L'Architecture d'aujourd'hui, 1983), p. 176, 512, 648, 714, 1023.

Elisabeth Allain-Dupré, "À la recherche de l'essentiel," *Le Moniteur architecture AMC*, No. 22, October 1988, p. 21–49.

James Read, "Yves Lion: Modernism in the Service of the City," *Architecture Today*, No. 11, 1990, p. 50–57.

Anne Demerle Got, "Profession: une agence sur mesures," *Le Moniteur architecture AMC*, No. 14, September 1990, p. 46–49.

Jacques Lucan, "Nauwgezette experimenten, recente projecten van Yves Lion," *Archis*, No. 10, October 1991, p. 20–21.

Paris, la ville et ses projets, collection de dessins d'architecture et d'urbanisme du Pavillon de l'Arsenal (Paris: Pavillon de l'Arsenal, 1995), p. 18, 86, 137, 146, 173, 176.

Françoise Arnold, *Le logement collectif* (Paris: Éditions du Moniteur, 1996), *passim*.

Bruno Fortier, ed., *Métamorphoses parisiennes* (Liège: Pierre Mardaga, 1996), p. 32, 197.

Jacques Lucan, "Yves Lion," in: Jean-Paul Midant, ed., *Dictionnaire de l'architecture du XXe siècle* (Paris: Hazan/Institut français d'architecture, 1996), p. 540.

Catherine Clarisse, *Ma quête d'architecture, maquettes d'architecture* (Paris: Pavillon de l'Arsenal, 1999), p. 22, 50, 119.

Jean-Claude Garcias, "Yves Lion," *Dictionnaire des architectes* (Paris: Encyclopaedia universalis/Albin Michel, 1999), p. 397.

"Yves Lion," in: Carlo Olmo, ed., *Dizionario dell'architettura dell XX secolo* (Turin: Umberto Allemandi, 2000), vol. 4, p. 100–101.

Bertrand Lemoine, *Birkhäuser Architectural Guide France, 20th Century* (Basel/Berlin/Boston: Birkhäuser, 2000), *passim*.

Jacques Lucan, *Architecture en France 1940–2000, histoire et théories* (Paris: Éditions du Moniteur, 2001), *passim*.

Jean-Michel Léger, "Rêver, expérimenter, rectifier/comprendre: les aventures de la 'bande active'/Y. Lion architect," *Lieux communs*, No. 6, 2002, p. 19–46.

Articles and publications about individual projects

Competition for Les Halles, 1979

Marc Emery, "Consultation internationale sur le quartier des Halles à Paris," *L'Architecture d'aujourd'hui*, No. 208, April 1980, p. 16.

Law Courts Draguignan, 1978–1983

"Yves Lion, le palais de justice de Draguignan," *Architecture, mouvement, continuité*, No. 52–53, 1980, p. 124–127.

Jean-Louis Cohen, "Il Palazzo di Giustizia di Draguignan: Yves Lion," *Casabella*, No. 482, July/August 1982, p. 2–9.

"Yves Lion; Law Courts, Draguignan 1981," *International Architect*, No. 10, 1983, p. 39–41.

Housing Noisy-le-Grand, 1982–1986

"Entretien avec Yves Lion," *Le Moniteur architecture AMC*, No. 65, 1995, p. 50.

Artists' atelier complex, Passage de Flandre, 1983–1987

Ricky Burdett, "Artists' studios, Quai de la Seine, Paris, 1986," in: *Three French architects: Berger, Faloci, Lion* (Paris: Institut Français d'Architecture/London: 9H Gallery, 1987), p. 14–15.

Silvia Milesi, "Un edificio residenziale di Yves Lion e François Leclercq a Parigi: percorsi per artisti," *Casabella*, No. 541, December 1987, p. 38–39.

Jacques Lucan, "Des ensembles de logements dans la ville, savoir faire urbain," in: *Eau et gaz à tous les étages, Paris 100 ans de logement* (Paris: Pavillon de l'Arsenal, 1992), p. 210–211.

Vocational School, Saint-Quai-Portrieux, 1986–1988

Jean-Paul Robert, "Lycée hôtelier à Saint-Quai-Portrieux," *L'Architecture d'aujourd'hui*, No. 260, December 1988, p. 92- 93.

Alain Guiheux, *Architectures publiques* (Liège: Pierre Mardaga, 2000), p. 24.

Museum of Franco-American Cooperation, Blérancourt, 1986–1989

Elisabeth Allain-Dupré, "Blérancourt, le musée franco-américain," *Le Moniteur architecture AMC*, No. 4, 1989, p. 36–40.

"Un léger décalage," *L'Architecture d'aujourd'hui*, No. 266, December 1989, p. 64–66.

Christian Devillers, "Il Museo franco-americano di Blérancourt di Yves Lion e Alan Levitt," *Casabella*, No. 565, February 1990, p. 4–9

Laurence Allégret, *Musées* (Paris: Electa Moniteur, 1992), vol. 2, p. 96–99.

Marble Architectural Awards 1993, Carrare, Internazionale Marmi e Macchine, 1993, p. 43–49.

Conference Centre and Opera, Nantes, 1986–1992

Jean-Louis Cohen, "Tessiture e riflessi oceanici: Lion e Levitt a Nantes," *Casabella*, No. 592, July/August 1992, p. 4–6; in English: *Architecture Today*, No. 31, 1992, p. 26–29; in German: *Bauwelt*, Berlin, 15 January 1993; in Spanish: *Architectura Viva*, No. 28, January/February 1993, p. 86–91.

Pascale Joffroy, "Le palais des congrès de Nantes," *Le Moniteur architecture AMC*, No. 31, May 1992, p. 30–45.

Mies van der Rohe Award for European Architecture 1992 (Barcelona: Fundaciò Mies van der Rohe, 1993), p. 92–95

Housing, Villejuif, 1986–1992

"Wohnriegel in Villejuif bei Paris," *Bauwelt*, No. 28–29, 30 June 1993, p.1522–1525.

Carlos Verdaguer, "La banda activa: ZAC des Hautes Bruyères, Villejuif," *Arquitectura viva*, No. 36, May/June 1994, p. 74–77.

Pierre-Alain Croset, Silvia Milesi, "Bercy e Villejuif: due quartieri parigini a confronto," *Casabella*, No. 617, 1994, p. 26–39.

Jean-Michel Léger, Benoîte Decup-Pannier, *Chambre-bains et terrasse avec vue; évaluation de la 'bande active' à Villejuif, Y. Lion arch.*, Paris, IPRAUS/Plan construction et architecture, 1995.

Jean-Louis Cohen, Monique Eleb, *Paris, architecture 1900–2000* (Paris: Norma, 2000), p. 246–249.

Law Court, Lyons, 1982–1995

Jana McCann, "De staat van de rechtsstaat; nieuw gerechtsgebouw voor Lyon van Yves Lion en Alan Levitt," *Archis*, No. 12, December 1995, p. 35–41.

Jean-Claude Garcias, "Modernitas legis custos, Palais de Justice à Lyon," *Bulletin de l'Institut français d'architecture*, October 1995, p. 7–8.

Rémi Fourrier, "Le palais de justice de Lyon," *Le Moniteur architecture AMC*, No. 62–63, June/July 1995, p. 12–18.

Marc Bédarida, "Lione: la politica degli spazi pubblici," *Casabella*, No. 629, December 1995, p. 8–23.

Bertrand Lemoine, *100 monuments du XXème siècle; patrimoine et architecture de la France* (Paris: Éditions France Loisirs/Éditions du Patrimoine, 2000), p. 208–209.

"*Domus Demain*" and other housing studies, 1984–1987

Gustau Gili Galfetti, "*Domus Demain*, investigación sobre un habitat para los principios del siglo XXI," in: *Pisos pilotos: celulas domesticas experimentales* (Barcelona: Gustavo Gili, 1997), p. 46–51.

Office building, Porte d'Italie, 1989–1993

"Yves Lion, edificio de oficinas, Paris," *Catalogos de arquitectura contemporánea* (Barcelona: Gustavo Gili, 1994), p. 120–127.

Housing, Bercy, 1990–1995

La ZAC Bercy," *Casabella*, No. 581, uly/August 1991, p. 56–59.

rançoise Fromonot, "Entre rue t parc: une promenade à Bercy," *Architecture d'aujourd'hui*, No. 295, ctober 1994, p.72–79.

Le front de parc de Bercy," *Le Moniteur architecture AMC*, No. 57, ecember 1994, p.76–78.

uropean House of Photography, 990–1996

atherine Séron-Pierre, " Maison uropéenne de la Photographie," *e Moniteur architecture AMC*, lo. 69, March 1996, p. 28–35.

obert Barnes, "Paris: the European hotography Centre is now open," *rchitecture Today*, No. 72, October 996, p. 7–9.

ean-Paul Robert, "Le syndrome u patrimoine," *L'Architecture 'aujourd'hui*, No. 304, April 1996, . 43.

en Powell, "City Transformed: rban Architecture at the Beginning f the 21st Century," (London: aurence King, 2000), p. 168–173.

aint-Denis Plain, 1991–2002

ndré Lortie, "Paris-phérie: Plaine aint-Denis e il 'Grand axe,'" *asabella*, No. 596, 1992, p. 32–43.

Christophe Bayle, " La plaine de Saint-Denis se met au vert" and Sylvie Schaffer, "Sainte-Geneviève des Bois, une ZAC respectueuse de l'écologie urbaine," *Urbanisme*, No. 258, November 1992, p. 16–26.

Michel Corajoud, "La Plaine-Saint-Denis: eine neue Stadtkultur für die Arbeits-Peripherie," *Bauwelt*, No. 48, December 1993, p. 2630–2635.

Gilles Davoine, "La Plaine Saint-Denis, l'émergence d'une ville plurielle," *Le Moniteur architecture AMC*, No. 104, February 2000, p. 102–129.

"Plaine-Saint-Denis project 800 ha," *IN-EX Projects Customize No. 2: Review of Peripheral Architecture* (Basel/Berlin/Boston: Birkhäuser, 2001), p. 426–433 (interview with Yves Lion, conducted by Périphériques).

Maisons Phénix, 1993–1994

Jean-Claude Garcias, "Du multiple au mono-plus, maisons Phénix," *Bulletin de l'Institut français d'architecture*, No. 169, 1993, p. 7.

Elisabeth Allain-Dupré, "Phénix et ses maisons d'architecte," *Le Moniteur architecture AMC*, No. 41, May 1993, p. 7.

Competition for the Souks of Beirut, 1994

"Schneller Wiederaufbau?," *Werk, Bauen+Wohnen*, No. 11, November 1994, p. 43.

Residence Rue Liancourt, 1994–1995

Gilles Davoine, "Immeuble unifamilial Paris 14e," *Le Moniteur architecture AMC*, No. 79, April 1997, p. 26–31.

"Eine Familie in der rue Liancourt," *Bauwelt*, No. 11, 14 March 1997, p. 508–511.

Conversion of an office and residential building, Rue Boileau, 1994–1996

"Conversion de oficinas en viviendas, Paris" and "Vivendas mejor," *Architectura viva*, No. 67, 1997, p. 102–105.

Michel Lombardini et al., "Wohnen im Büro," *Bauwelt*, No. 31–32, 22 August 1997, p. 1720–1733.

Mies van der Rohe Award for European Architecture 1996 (Barcelona: Fundaciò Mies van der Rohe, 1997), p. 104–107.

Housing Quai Henri IV, 1994–1998

Jean-Claude Garcias, "La caserne enchantée, logements à Paris," *Bulletin de l'Institut français d'architecture*, No. 213, 1998, p. 9.

Sebastian Redecke, "Wohnen an der Seine," *Bauwelt*, No. 35, 17 September 1999, p. 1904–1909.

Conversion of an office and residential building, Boulevard de Grenelle, 1995–1997

Raymond Fachette, Corinne Jaquand, "La reconversion de bureaux en logements," *Urbanisme*, No. 294, June 1997, p. 36–40.

Didot-Thermopyles quarter, 1997–1998

"Didot Thermopyles," *Quartiers anciens, approches nouvelles, Paris Projet*, No. 32–33, p. 138–143

French Embassy in Beirut, Lebanon, 1997–2003

A. Trad, "Les nouvelles voies de la sérénité," *Déco magazine, architecture & design*, February 2003, p. 96–99.

Frédéric Edelmann, "À Beyrouth, un éclat de pierre venu de France," *Le Monde*, 18–19 January 2004, p. 21.

Jean-Pierre Cousin, "Ambassade de France, Beyrouth, Liban," *L'Architecture d'aujourd'hui*, No. 351, March/April 2004, p. 14–15.

Design: Binocular, New York

A CIP catalogue record for this book is available from the Library of Congress, Washington D.C., USA

Bibliographic information published by Die Deutsche Bibliothek. Die Deutsche Bibliothek lists this publication in the Deutsche Nationalbibliografie; detailed bibliographic data is available in the internet at http://dnb.ddb.de.

Illustration credits

All illustrations not listed are by Ateliers Lion architectes urbanistes.

Jean-Louis Cohen: 11 (top row)

Gitty Darugar: 2, 41 (top), 83, 84, 85, 86, 93, 94, 95, 97 (top), 98, 122, 124 (bottom), 145 (top), 152

Philippe Hersaut: 53 (middle)

Adrià Goula Sarda: 9 (bottom), 57, 58/59, 61, 62, 63, 100, front cover

Yves Lion: 31 (bottom), 44, 45, 46

Jean-Marie Monthiers: 5, 9 (top), 22 (top), 23, 24, 25, 36, 37, 41 (bottom), 42, 48, 49, 53 (bottom), 68, 69, 70/71, 72, 73, 75, 78, 79, 80, 81 (top), 87, 91 (bottom left), 97 (bottom), 99, 101 (top), 123, 125

Jean-Marie Monthiers and Gaston Bergeret: 74, 76/77, back cover

Jacques Péré: 11 (bottom) (from the book: *David Georges Emmerich*, éditions HYX 1997)

Dahliette Sucheyre: 15 (top), 19 (bottom), 35 (bottom), 121

Daniel Tajan: 13 (bottom)

Techniques et Architecture (N° 311, Oct./Nov. 1976): 40

Printed on acid-free paper produced from chlorine-free pulp. TCF ∞

Printed in Germany
ISBN – 13 978-3-7643-6301-7
ISBN – 10 3-7643-6301-0

9 8 7 6 5 4 3 2 1

www.birkhauser.ch